MOMMY DRUNKEST

*How Losing My Little Angels
Freed Me Of My Demons*

Brittany Priestley

Forward by Adam Vibe Gunton

MOMMY DRUNKEST

Copyright © 2020 by Recovered On Purpose

All rights reserved. No part of this publication may be reproduced, distributed, or transmitted in any form or by any means, including photocopying, recording, or other electronic or mechanical methods, without the prior written permission of the publisher, except in the case of brief quotations embodied in reviews and certain other non-commercial uses permitted by copyright law.

Some names and identifying details have been changed to protect the privacy of individuals.

For information contact :
Brittany Priestley at MommyDrunkestOfficial@gmail.com

Cover design by Classiquedesign
Classiquedesign001@gmail.com

Edited and formatted by Jessica Granillo
https://GranilloEditorial.com

CONTENTS

1. MY ROAD TO HELL WAS PAVED WITH GOOD INTENTIONS
2. COLD
3. THE SANDBOX
4. HANDCUFFS
5. CONTROL
6. UNWORTHY
7. LIGHTNESS BY WAY OF LIQUID
8. DRUG
9. ONE HUNDRED DAYS
10. THE MORTICIAN'S HOUSE
11. NO SMOKING ALLOWED
12. MOMMY DRUNKEST
13. GETTING AWAY WITH IT
14. HOMELESS
15. UNEXPECTED GUARDIAN ANGEL
16. KALEIDOSCOPE EYES
17. DEMONS ARE HERE; THE END IS NEAR
18. TWENTY MONTHS WITHOUT A HEART
19. COURTROOM PRAYER
20. PURPOSE OF GOD'S IMPECCABLE TIMING

To My Mom and Dad (Bird)

For giving me unconditional love, so I, in turn, could give love unconditionally to my own children.

To Avonlea, Finn, River, and Cambria

*For being, by far, my greatest blessings.
For being my saving grace. I love you all, from here, to eternity, and back again.*

To My Heavenly Father

For your many blessings—the ones I am deeply grateful for, the ones I didn't realize I had, the ones yet to come. For my beautiful children. For everything.

"You," he said, *"are a terribly real thing in a terribly false world, and that, I believe, is why you are in so much pain."*
    -Emilie Autumn

FORWARD

COURAGE. STRENGTH. HOPE. That is what you will find inside the stories within Brittany's book: *Mommy Drunkest*. So many addicts and alcoholics in recovery have amazing testimonies of overcoming some of the most troubling circumstances imaginable in a human life.

It is time these stories are shared with the world in a powerful way that will not only help society, or "normies," understand some of the circumstances involved with becoming full-blown addicts, but also to share a message of hope to those still suffering from addiction.

One month after publishing my book: *From Chains To Saved*, I attended a conference in San Diego, California. I was standing in the back of the room, watching the stage, when a young man I had never met approached me with a copy of my book he had bought online and said, "Bro, your book changed my life. I have three weeks clean. Will you sign it for me?" The feeling I had in that moment, as if a life had been changed by me simply sharing my story, was one I will never forget and one I have since wanted to share with as many recovered addicts and alcoholics as possible. And that is why I started Recovered On Purpose, and how Brittany and I met.

I knew there was something special about her story the first time I spoke with her over a video call. Her daughter was running around in the background. She had a smile on her face the entire time we talked. She radiated a certain type of *knowing* that only comes from someone who has *been through it* and made it out on the other side. Gratitude.

As I got to know Brittany and her story more and more through the Recovered On Purpose Pain To Purpose Program, it dawned on me like never before that her story is going to reach an audience in a way that mine may never have been able to. With her unique story of overcoming her childhood traumas, issues with identity, worthiness, and addictions ultimately leading to losing her children, she gives hope to so many women I have seen in recovery that are fighting the uphill battle of getting their children back from the system that took them due to their active addictions.

Her story will give hope to anyone in recovery or struggling in active addiction but will also show the world the battle faced by addicts and alcoholics every single day. It has been an honor and a privilege to be a part in showing her the way to write her story. But, ultimately, she sat down and made the decision that she wanted to get it out to help as many people as possible and who knows where this is now going to go.

If you are reading this, prepare yourself for a journey of pain, emotions, confusion, growth, and triumph that will ultimately lead to a message of hope for you to get clean, share your story, and live Recovered On Purpose.

Humbly Yours,
Adam Vibe Gunton
Founder: Recovered On Purpose

"Cling to the thought that, in God's hands, the dark past is the greatest possession you have—the key to life and happiness for others. With it you can avert death and misery for them."

-Big Book of Alcoholics Anonymous

CHAPTER ONE

My Road to Hell was Paved with Good Intentions

I HAVE ALWAYS HAD AN affinity for children; for those who were not prepared to care for themselves, who needed guidance and protection. Anyone, really, who was susceptible to vulnerability, still in possession of their innocence, and needed a voice to speak up for them when all they could manage was to remain silent. I had this connection with children.

Whenever I looked at them, I could see myself

as I really was, or who I was meant to be. I could sense the child in me reaching out for guidance and protection. In need of an allowance or some sort of permission to be heard, and to be vulnerable with no trace of shame or guilt.

In an attempt to protect myself, this damaged girl, who wanted nothing more than to be buried deep, I started building a fortress. First, I spread mortar around my heart, made with grains of sand and cemented with trepidation. As each piece of me crumbled, a new stone was laid. As time passed, my fortress became strong and sturdy, with each new hurt, each heartbreak, and every unkind word strengthening the wall. The stone spiraled, surrounding my heart, and new walls rose from my center point, becoming intertwined with every morsel of me. It kept me protected and safe from intruders and anyone or anything trying to invade my space with malicious intent.

Trespassers beware of the rage building up behind my walls. Rage designed to be catapulted with fiery fury through the air in an attempt to scare them away. And atop that wall, entwined with barbed wire, me behind it, my icy aloofness and blank stare, looking right through my attackers like they never existed at all.

While keeping others out, I caged myself in. It became lonely living in my own head, behind indestructible walls no one could get through and that I, myself, could not escape.

I never wanted any child to experience a small part of themselves dying or crumbling, where an inner brokenness would dwell, as it did in myself. I wished I could protect every single one of them. Children always felt comfortable with me. I believe they could see a part of themselves in me, too. I worked with children for a long time. I loved them as if they were my own. I always knew I wanted to have children of my own. I knew I'd be a mother.

When I did become a mother, I had so many visions of what my life with my children would look like. I wanted my kids to remain free-spirited and carefree. I wanted them to hold on to their innocence as long as humanly possible. I felt I had a clean slate, and with it, I could help guide and encourage my children to become the best parts of me. They would overshadow that little girl I didn't allow to step out from behind the walls, and into the sunlight. I wanted them to grow to their upmost potential and never feel the need to hide.

I was not going to let what happened to me, happen to them. That was one thing I was sure of. I had an awareness and a knowledge of people. I could sense a creep from a hundred miles away. This ability came about when I was young. I believe the abuse I endured opened up the world and universe to me. I was given the gift of sight, an inner knowing, a heightened intuition. I am grateful for it now, but I haven't always been. I kept my kids close. I only allowed people I loved and truly trusted to be around them, especially alone. I vowed to keep their self-worth intact. They would be able to love themselves, if only I could protect them from the perversions of the world.

In theory, this sounded splendid. I may have shielded them from one set of horrible events that take place in life. I may have saved them from the trauma I had experienced. I just didn't quite realize that my unhealed heart, with the best of intentions, would introduce new cycles of dysfunction that would later need to be broken. I tried to protect them from the devils of the world.

All the while, the devil was sitting at my kitchen table, with a chilled glass of straight whiskey in his hoof. He was always sitting idly by, waiting for me. I tried to keep outsiders from coming in, all the while keeping my most beloved caged close to my heart. I kept them trapped with me in my state of fear, huddled together and enclosed, in my spiraling fortress.

I did have the best of intentions for my children. I did not have the best of intentions for myself. Therein lies the problem. I needed to begin healing, stop hiding, become bare and vulnerable; only then could I be a helping guide for my kids and for myself. I wasted a lot of time protecting them from my fears of what could happen, as opposed to protecting them from what was actually happening. They were witnesses to the ugliness that comes, bottle in hand, from having two parents suffering from alcoholism and addiction.

I pray they now know that no matter what, I have and will always love them more than anything. I pray they realize that nothing was ever their fault. In no way could they have helped our situation, and in no way were they ever responsible. I pray they know their worth is immeasurable. To God, they were made perfectly the way He intended them to be. I pray they know the amount of gratitude I have to God for gifting them to me. They are my most cherished treasures, my little angels.

Yes, I did always have the best intentions, but I sure did pave and drive the road down towards hell, everyone kept safe, strapped into their seatbelts. It wasn't until I lost my angels, along the way, that I was able to find my inner child. I gave her a big hug and told her we would be alright. I needed to be freed from the self-restraints I had bound myself with, my cage, and from myself. I needed to be freed from my addictions. I desperately needed freedom from all my demons.

BRITTANY PRIESTLEY

MOMMY DRUNKEST

"I hope she'll be a fool—that's the best thing a girl can be in this world, a beautiful little fool."
　　- F. Scott Fitzgerald

CHAPTER TWO

Cold

AS MOST LITTLE GIRLS DO, I admired the older girls who wore makeup, had cool clothes, and seemed to be and have everything I wanted. Imagine my astonishment when two girls, fitting this image perfectly, invited me over to their house to play one day. I was beyond excited. I asked my mom if I could go. She replied yes. She bundled me up. I ran out the front door and skipped across the street.

Their voices carried from the backyard. I called out, "Hello!" They told me to come in through the gate. I placed both feet on a wooden plank to hoist myself up. I reached up, on my tip toes, to unlock the latch on the wood gate from the other side. I hopped down, pushed open the gate, and trekked through the snow.

When I looked up, those two pretty, untouchable girls were hanging out of the first story window. They called me over to the window, and I excitedly obeyed, wanting to hear anything they had to say to me. They glanced at each other and then back down to me. They told me they had something they wanted to give me. This could not get any better. They both reached back into the house and held out a gift that I reached out for, with opened arms extended. With that, a bucket full of cold water drenched me from head to toe, cascading down my body and hitting the snow. Shocked, stunned, frozen; I heard them giggle and then they called me a name I'd never heard before. They called me a slut.

I don't remember trudging back home. I don't recall walking through my front door. I don't recall what I said to my mom, if I even told her what happened. I just remember laying in layers and layers of blankets on my mother's bed watching her organize drawers. It seemed as if I stayed curled up in that position for hours. My only thoughts were, "What did I do wrong and what was that name they called me?"

When I talked to my mom about this incident, just recently, she remembered it. She had been angry with those girls and had every intention to go and have a talk with their mothers. She told me my reaction was strange for someone my age. She told me I cried, "No! Don't! It will just make it worse."

Warmth was all I wanted. I had never felt this kind of cold. Much later I would realize those girls had crushes on some of the older boys in the neighborhood. Those same boys had taken a liking to me. I was three years old.

MOMMY DRUNKEST

"The most important decision we make is whether we believe we live in a friendly or hostile universe."
      -Albert Einstein

CHAPTER THREE

The Sandbox

THE FIRST HOME THAT I lived in was really ideal. We lived in a suburb just south of Salt Lake City, Utah, surrounded by beautiful mountain ranges. We lived on a street where everyone knew each other, some better than others. Overall, the families on that street spent a lot of time together. My mom and dad made close friends with the other men and women in the neighborhood, and in turn their kids all became friends.

It was a warm day. A bunch of the neighborhood kids were playing outside. We all had free reign on Dusty Creek Lane. I would pull my Teddy Ruxpin in my little red wagon along with Rainbow Brite, and various other stuffed animals. The older kids rode their bikes and skateboards up and down our street. My favorite was my Little Tikes car. It was the kind where I had to use my feet to get going, like in The Flintstone's. We would race each other, and needless to say, I never won. That didn't matter to me. I was one of the youngest kids living on our street, and I was just happy to be included.

We decided to spend that day at my house. There was a large wood deck on the back of our house with a view of those beautiful mountain ranges. Our backyard was large, so there was lots of room for us to run and play. Our dog, a Golden Lab named Champ, would run and play with us. Compared to little me, he was huge, and I used to ride on his back pretending he was my horse. A bunch of us were running up and down the deck steps, into the house through the sliding glass door, and then back out again. My mom had given us ice cream, and we were trying to get a little more. I remember I was so happy and care-free. There were mostly boys, my older brother's friends, and a few girls.

Under the stairs of the deck was a sandbox my dad had built. I loved playing in there. It was kind of enclosed, so it was a sandbox that doubled as a fort. The boys decided we should go into the sandbox and play. We all piled in and sat wherever we could fit. I wondered what we would do. When I played in there I pretended it was a house or I would draw designs in the sand. Honestly, most of the time, I sat in there and ate the sand. I don't know why, but I loved the taste and crunch of it.

One boy named Teeg had an idea. Teeg was eleven or twelve, about nine years older than me. He was the type of kid that was rough around the edges. He was more on the bad side than on the good. He was skinny and not well kept, usually downright dirty. His father was strange. We rarely saw him and he had very little to no interaction with any of the other parents. I didn't like Teeg. Not one bit. He was mean, especially towards me. Just a few days earlier he had trapped me inside the barbecue in his backyard. He shut the lid on me and wouldn't let me out. I felt weary and uncomfortable around him. He scared me.

I wasn't paying much attention, kind of in my own world, when everyone got quiet. "Has anyone ever seen a vagina?" he asked. Everyone just kind of sat there, and slowly all the other kids shook their heads no. "Do you guys want to see one?" he asked, looking over at me.

Oh my, how I wished that sandbox was filled with quicksand so I could just sink right down to the center of the earth. He inched towards me. I knew what he wanted and what he was going to do. He slid my skirt up past my narrow hips, exposing my My Little Pony panties. He slid them down and I instinctively squeezed my knees together. He slid them over my knees and left them at my ankles. He told me to open. I sat there bare and utterly exposed. I sat there with my skirt up over my hips and my panties down around my ankles and I couldn't move. I was petrified. There was a group of kids, my friends, staring at me and I couldn't move. On the outside I was stone, but inside I was crumbling.

He said he wondered what it felt like. He opened my legs and everyone just stared. I don't even remember looking at their faces. I could just feel them. I made no sound until he stuck his finger inside me. I inhaled sharply, but made no other sound. It just hurt so badly. "It feels weird and squishy," he said as he moved his sand and dirt encrusted fingers inside me. When he was done he smelled his fingers and had everyone else smell them. He then he put his fingers under my nose.

I couldn't name the emotion that I felt, all I knew was it didn't feel right and something was very wrong. I was bad. I felt dirty, and it wasn't this cruel boy's uncleanliness that made me feel that way. This was not supposed to happen on this beautiful day with my friends, in the sandbox I sometimes pretended was my home.

I don't remember the other kids leaving. I don't remember pulling my panties up and my skirt down. I know I sat there for a while. I still didn't move or make a sound. I don't even think I cried. That was the day I started building walls of brick and stone around me, to protect me from others and to prevent myself from crumbling. I put on a brave face.

I lost something that day. I lost my childish innocence, although I would still fake it for years and years to come. Once I finally stood up and walked away, I didn't look back and I never stepped foot in that sandbox again.

MOMMY DRUNKEST

"Father, forgive them, for they know not what they do." Luke 23:24
-Jesus Christ

CHAPTER FOUR

Handcuffs

THROUGHOUT MY LIFE I HAVE found myself in an array of various peculiar scenes. Years later they would play in my mind, like snippets from a movie. Some were funny, some just outright strange, and some were scary. For a long time I would hit the rewind button and replay these memories over and over and over again in my mind.

With some memories, I was longing for the happiness and peace I had once felt. Other times, I was wondering if I could have done anything to change a sequence of events that had taken place. Most of the time, I was wishing things had not taken place at all. I was falling into the trap of what ifs, and more specifically, who would I be now if I hadn't had that experience? Really, there is no need to ponder such things, because no answer exists. What is, is what is and what was, it was. The past cannot be changed.

One afternoon, around the same time as the sandbox incident, I found myself alone with one of the older neighborhood boys in the basement of his house. I was three at the time and he was about twelve. He was not babysitting me, so I've often wondered how we ended up there. There were no other kids around, and his parents and sister were not home. This boy was different; I thought he was really cute. I liked him. A lot of the girls liked him.

In his basement there was a bedroom. The bedroom belonged to his parents. I still remember a big bed, the color maroon, nice furniture, and a fireplace. Very romantic. He laid me on the bed. He began kissing me using his tongue. It wasn't much longer before he stopped and got up. I did not know what the hell was going on. I felt something was definitely wrong. We shouldn't be doing this. I shouldn't be here. Where is everyone? I should get up and go home. All these thoughts ran through my mind. Before I had the chance to make any sort of movement or decision, he walked back into the bedroom. He was holding a pair of handcuffs.

Up until that point, I had never seen handcuffs. Not even a set of play handcuffs. He intended these for play, but they were the real deal. I had no idea what he was planning to do with them or with me. I just froze while he held my left wrist up, and hooked it to the bed post. At this, I moved awkwardly, and he whispered, "Shh, just relax," and proceeded with my right wrist. I was stuck. Now there was no getting up, there was no going home. I still wasn't sure what the hell was going on, and both of my tiny wrists were handcuffed to a bed in the basement of a house.

I do not know how much time passed. I know I was kissed a lot. He had pulled my pants down and explored my body with his hands. He laid on top of me. He was gentle. I went somewhere else. I felt like I had to escape into my own mind. I didn't put up a fight or scream, but I do remember trying to squirm away and put some space between the two of us. I don't remember him taking the handcuffs off. Maybe someone came home or someone came looking for me, I have no clue. He may have just been done with me. I don't remember getting up from that bed or walking out of that room.

I wouldn't tell anyone about this experience for another thirteen years, drunk at a friend's house party. I was finally able to let it leave my head and express it out loud. I had kept the memory contained and a bottle of liquor allowed me to find the right words to spit it out. Alcohol made me brave. Alcohol made me feel like I could open up, finally, after years of being closed off and hiding behind the fortress I had built from stones made of shame and guilt. Alcohol gave me relief.

My family moved from Utah to Southern California when I was five. Every summer, my family and I made the twelve hour drive to visit our old friends. I was always so anxious to go back to our old street. I would see that boy and all the other neighborhood kids. My heart would just race. The summer I turned eight, I was sitting at a friend's kitchen table during our annual visit. She was a few years older than me. She was catching me up on the neighborhood gossip and mentioned Teeg.

At that point, I knew what had happened in the sandbox was wrong. I knew, because events similar to these kept happening to me in California—in a different state and a different neighborhood. Same me. I was older and I knew it was bad. I told her how I felt about it, that I felt wronged and used. She shook her head, "No, you wanted him to finger bang you." What? I had never heard that term before and wouldn't hear it again or understand what it meant for another four years. I didn't believe it, but she did. I must have asked for it. It was all my fault. I was defective, I was tainted. Things like this don't keep happening to good girls.

Growing up, the subject of boys came up often with my friends. I would instantly freeze up and get nervous. They would recount stories of their first kisses. They would tell cute stories about a boy that had pecked them on the lips when they were twelve, or about an innocent kiss on the playground. I would sit there, stomach knotted, trying to make up some acceptable story, never thinking that I should just tell the truth. To me, the truth was I wasn't innocent. I was wrong, I was bad. I was so ashamed and so embarrassed. My first kiss was in that basement, handcuffed to a bed.

MOMMY DRUNKEST

Who?

Alone with so many people around
I hear my own laughter
But I'm not making a sound
Looking around thinking there's nothing to say
Words flow from my mouth like every other day
Outside I'm smiling, inside I'm crying
With difficulty to keep my emotions inside
My fears try to escape my heart and hide
My head will find them, alright
When I find myself asleep at night
A different world where everything is dealt
Finally, the clarity I see is myself
I've heard you are the only person who truly knows you
What if that is what the truth was
But if you don't, then who does

CHAPTER FIVE

Control

THE NEED TO CONTROL CREPT up early in my life. I guess you could say it made me feel secure. I had to remain in control in a world that was unpredictable and felt completely out of control. Other people were my first obstacle, and I noticed myself trying to steer and bend them to my will. When friends would come over to play, I imposed my ideas and wants onto them. We would do what I wanted to do, play what I wanted to play, and listen to music I wanted to listen to. If and when a friend wanted to leave, I wouldn't let them. I would block the door, keeping them trapped in my bedroom, coercing them to stay. Why anyone ever remained my friend or decided to play with me again, I will never know. I had a need to dominate and it followed me like a shadow everywhere I went.

Perfectionism was another form of control that I used against myself. Whatever I did, I had to be the best. If I knew I wasn't going to be the best, I would forfeit. This trait made me an excellent student. I was in honor classes. I got good grades, usually straight A's. I'd beat myself up over a B. I loved my teachers and they loved me. I'd get special recognition and awards. I felt that if I put out this facade of perfection and achievement into the world, then somehow, I would begin to feel better about myself. I'd magically transform my perfect grades and perfect attendance into something that resembled self worth.

I had a lot of friends. I only had a few that I let get really close to me, to see the parts of me that were imperfect. I also had a lot of enemies. I noticed that people usually either loved me or they really disliked me. I was quiet and standoffish to people I didn't know. Some thought me a snob. Some people bought my portrayal of perfection mixed with a whole lot of false pride.

Internally, I was consumed with feelings of unworthiness, self-hatred, insecurity, fear, ad infinitum. I had too many feelings, and I did not know how to handle them. I saved my sensitive, sweet side for the few people I trusted. I had a deep loyalty and love for anyone I kept close to my heart; and if you pledged your allegiance to me, I'd walk to the ends of the earth for you.

In the sixth grade I realized people really didn't like to be controlled. My dominance caused some retaliation from the people I knew. I discovered there was something I could have complete authority over—food. Food didn't talk back, didn't resist, and did as it was told. I could do with it as I pleased. I could eat as much or as little as I wanted, or I could leave it alone altogether. I was not the type to eat my feelings. I wanted to starve them, let them shrivel up until they were nothing. I had always been a picky eater. My mom's dad, Grandpa Ed, gave me the nickname, "Little Miss Finicky." Even my pickiness was to the extreme, as most everything tended to be in my life. That being said, refusing food didn't appear to be too out of the ordinary for the people around me.

The restriction came on slowly. I would cut out meals and I began to run again. A few years before I had run track on a children's team for Florence Griffith Joyner, also known as Flo Jo. She had held the world record for the 100 meter dash. I had done well and won some first place medals for short distance. Now when I ran, I strove for long distance. It would burn more calories. I even started taking diet pills to curb my appetite.

People would tell me how tiny I was in a complimentary tone. I grew up in Orange County, California where outside appearances were everything. I was receiving positive reinforcement and attention for my securely hidden destructive behavior. And all the while I was maintaining my need to manage something. It was perfect.

A new internal struggle was born—my need for food as nourishment and survival, and my disgust with it. My obsessive control over food made me hate food. I hated it, because I needed it and I didn't want to be dependent on anything. I hated it, because I was deathly afraid of being fat. If that happened then my outside wouldn't seem perfect and it would match my inner ugliness.

No matter how many bones I could see, or vertebrae I could count, it was never enough. I would stand in front of the mirror and feel utterly repulsed by my disgusting reflection. I would poke and pinch at my skin to determine how much fat was still there, just lurking under the surface waiting to show itself. I sought validation through my appearance.

Ever since I was three years old, I battled with hating the shell I felt trapped in, my body. Some believe our bodies to be our temples. I learned mine was not sacred. I learned that when people started touching my body without asking, like it wasn't my decision. It didn't belong to me, and it was built for others to have and control.

I had the illusion of control, but in reality my mind was the thing spinning out of control. It was only going to get worse. Imagine the chaos that would ensue once my made-to-order cocktail of drugs and alcohol starting poisoning my already addled mind. All the things I ever tried to mold, contort, or control always backfired. Every one of those things got a steadfast grip on me, and obtained complete dominion over my life.

MOMMY DRUNKEST

"God has given you one face and you make yourself another."
    -William Shakespeare

CHAPTER SIX

Unworthy

THE DAY I WAS BAPTIZED holds a special place in my heart. I understood evil existed in the world. I had witnessed and been participant to the ugliness humans inflicted on one another. I knew there were dark figures that lurked in lonely spaces. I could feel darkness. Where there is darkness, then nearby, there surely must be some light. It was easier for me to sense the darkened crevices and chinks in shiny armor that were meant to protect, than it was for me to see the eminence of a simple prayer that held the power to do just that.

MOMMY DRUNKEST

Leading up to my baptism I met with the bishop of our church, and he gave me lessons in preparation for that day. I would be washed of my sins and accept the Father, Jesus Christ, and the Holy Ghost into my heart, life, and spirit. I understood whole-heartedly the commitment I was making. I always knew there was something more, a Power of Good that was almighty and superseded people here on earth, whatever is out in the universe, and everything evil. I felt a connection to that source, God.

Most of my father's side of the family are members of The Church of Jesus Christ of Latter-Day Saints. My Grandpa Priestley was very active in the church, and served missions in both England and Scotland. He sang in church with a deep, bellowing voice, which sometimes embarrassed me. He owned his own organ and played the organ in church. My Grandma Priestley was also devout. I was the youngest grandchild on that side of the family, and I was her favorite. She doted on me. She kept a white stuffed kitten at her house that no one but me was allowed to touch. She made me feel special. She often read those books, *Scary Stories to Tell in the Dark*, to me. Along with my connection to her, I felt weirdly connected to all things scary, other-worldly, and not of this realm. I found it odd that my grandma told me those stories at such a young age, not because they scared me, but more specifically due to her religious standing. Perhaps she knew something I did not know at the time.

She died of dementia when I was ten. The last few times I saw her, she looked like an entirely different person, and the grandma I loved was no longer there. She did not know who I was. She kept a picture of me in her room at the care facility where she lived until her death. My Grandma Priestley's death was the first loss I ever experienced. For years I would pray to God about her, and from time to time I still do. I would later come to realize she did remember me, and I felt her presence around me after her death. She would come and visit my childhood home. She would turn on an old lamp that once belonged to her any time I would sit in the office to read. I saw her walking throughout my house, where she used to visit every year.

My dad was an active member of the LDS church as well. He was ordained with the Melchizedek Priesthood, "the power of godliness is manifest" (Doctrine and Covenants 84:20). Genesis introduces Melchizedek—a "priest of God most High," as he blesses Abram.

The day I was baptized, it was by my father's hands. I was eight years old and dressed in an all white jumpsuit the church had prepared for me to wear. The water felt so warm and comforting as we took the steps into the baptismal spa, and the water came up about waist high. I was nervous with excitement. My dad raised his right hand and held onto my right wrist, my hands overlapping his. He began to immerse me completely into the water, but my right leg shot straight up out of the water. I have never been one to do anything easily. He pushed my leg back down, and began to immerse me again saying, "Having been commissioned of Jesus Christ, I baptize you in the name of the Father, and of the Son, and of the Holy Ghost. Amen."

In that moment I felt clean. I felt warmth and peace. After my mom helped me dry my hair and put on my pretty dress, we walked down the ward hallway into a room full of people. People from the church and some family members were in attendance. I sat down on a cushioned chair in the middle of the room.

My dad began blessing me with the laying on of

hands, giving me my confirmation. I sat there with my eyes shut, and a sensation of love and warmth came over me. Once again, there was that peace. It was a rippling of energy that began in the middle of my chest and spread out in every direction, shooting out of my body and encompassing me. I had been given and received the gift of the Holy Spirit. I felt eternal love.

My dad looked down to me and asked, "How do you feel?" I could not portray the feeling I experienced with words so I replied, "Warm and tingly." He smiled. Deep down though, I felt something else. I felt a faint weariness. Doubt was present too. I probably wouldn't have noticed it if I had been able to appreciate that moment for what it was, but it wouldn't take long for me to feel unclean once again.

I felt fulfilled and whole in my relationship with God, Jesus Christ, and the Holy Spirit. I held them dear and close to my heart. From the start, I held my spirituality close to me like a child who held onto a safety blanket in a dark bedroom. I wanted it to protect me and I wanted to keep it protected from people. As far as I was concerned, people tended to ruin things they got their hands on.

MOMMY DRUNKEST

How I felt about God was an entirely different thing then how I felt about church. At church I felt empty. I felt like an outcast. I felt stupid. I felt alone. My dad always took me and my second oldest brother most Sundays. My mom didn't attend church with us. She was either working or she didn't want to go, and I never knew why. My oldest brother and I have different fathers, and he lived in Utah near his father.

Not having my entire family there, I felt further separated from the rest of the congregation. All the families seemed so perfect in their Sunday best with everyone in tow. I knew my family was not perfect, it wasn't even close, and I so wanted perfection. So many times I would look at the other children and think how lucky they were to be so innocent and good. I envied them.

I knew too much about the wrong kinds of things and too little about what was good and right. I knew too much about boys, or they knew too much about me. I saw things and heard things that other people didn't seem to see or hear. I felt things. I felt things too damn much, always bombarded by feelings all around me. I knew things I shouldn't have known, seemingly coming from nowhere.

There were a lot of times I knew what people were thinking. I thought I was insane. Now I know that not to be the case, at least partially. I guess you could call it heightened intuition. Whatever it was, I did not understand it. Most of the time, humans are scared of things we cannot comprehend. I was scared of these experiences as well as confused by them. Still, there were other things I saw that perplexed and terrified me. I saw them awake, but I would be visited mostly at night.

Since I was a child I've woken up at some time during the hour of three o'clock in the morning, on a nightly basis. This still happens to me today. Sometimes I thought I was having really horrible nightmares, but they were too vivid, too real. They were palpable. I tried telling the adults in my life about all the things I didn't understand with the expectation that they would help me. I tried sleeping in my parents' bed, and when that wasn't allowed, I'd sleep on the floor next to their bed. I was only ever told I had a vivid imagination. So much for telling people your deepest darkest secrets and fears. I just ended up with no validation for the way I was feeling or comfort from what was happening to me, at least from people. I did pray, and I kept a picture of Jesus by my bed I would look at and hold onto in these times of duress.

The girls at church tried to get to know me, but I wouldn't let them get too close. I didn't want to contaminate them. I spent a lot of time falsely believing they had shunned me and pushed me away, because they thought they were better than me. The truth was I thought they were better than me. Resentment and the art of blame came early for me, along with the habit of lying to myself. I stopped attending church when I was thirteen.

At this time I found out I had an older half sister that my parents had kept a secret. Before my parents had met, my dad dated a woman and got her pregnant. The woman's father wouldn't allow my dad to be in their lives if he didn't marry her. When my sister was old enough to reach out, she sent a letter in the mail to my dad. I found the letter and read it. That was how I found out. I felt betrayed and lied to by the people I trusted most.

Around this time, I also started drinking alcohol and smoking weed more often. These substances gave me comfort when I needed it. I could shut down my brain for a little while. I could find ease and relief. Those feelings were good, but they did not compare to the warm, tingling, true feeling of peace I felt when my father's hands lay on my head and the Holy Spirit was shielding me. Even so, I turned my back on the church, full of its judgmental, hypocritical, perfect people and began swiftly down the road towards the worship of other things. Things that would give me what I wanted, when I wanted them. After all, the belief in my unworthiness surpassed any and all of my other beliefs by miles.

Warning

I put myself through rigorous deception
Make me think there's that special connection
People's actions teach me a very good lesson
They will walk all over you if you let them
So heighten that wall and harden your heart
If you wear it on your shoulder it could all fall apart
Don't give in and tell them your secrets
You can see in his eyes the power he gets
All I can say is once they know
They'll make it entertainment and put on a show

CHAPTER SEVEN

Lightness by Way of Liquid

SIPS OF BUDWEISER FROM MY dad's beer bottle always tasted bitter. I did not like the taste, but I did like the lightness I felt when I drank it. My dad was not an alcoholic, but on holidays and at family gatherings he would partake. Even though the taste didn't appeal to me, I would continue asking for more sips and then make my rounds to other family members. They thought it was cute that I, an eight-year-old at the time, wanted to be included in the fun. No harm done.

My mom and her friends enjoyed each other's

company sitting around a table with chilled glasses full of wine. I would sit with them, listening to their stories and laughter. I felt comfortable and safe sitting with these women, just listening and sipping on wine. There was that elusive feeling of lightness again that came with every sip I swallowed. I remember I would get a little tipsy on a few of these occasions. I was giddy and lighthearted. I felt as though I was free from myself, outside of my own head for a short while. I felt care-free, like I expected a child was supposed to feel. Moments like this were few and far between, so I relished the feeling, the atmosphere, the connectivity, and the camaraderie. I wasn't so isolated in a world of my own. This was a different world, less hostile and more enjoyable.

    I was left home alone quite often. My parents worked and my older brother had better things to do than watch his little sister. My parents kept their liquor under the cabinet of our bar, which was hardly ever used for that purpose. My mom usually left stacks of paper and mail in the sink, rendering it useless.

    Like I said, my parents weren't big drinkers. I believe they could possibly be members of the few elite that are actually able to learn from the mistakes of others. They both learned painful lessons that deterred them from ever going overboard. Both my mother and my father had brothers who were alcoholics, and both committed suicide.

My dad always told me I reminded him of his brother when I drank, and I never knew how to take that. His brother became mean and violent. He told me his eyes would turn completely black.

He committed suicide before I was born, but I always felt a connection to him. I would see his spirit too. It scared me that I felt I could understand him, because I really could. My Grandpa Priestley was the one that found his body. He was in his garage with the door closed and the engine running. He didn't find him sitting in the car. He found him on the ground by the garage door with a bloody face and his nose badly broken. He didn't want to end his life. He changed his mind. That story always haunted me and I believe it saved my life on quite a few occasions.

On these days when I was left to my own devices, with no homework to do and no friends around to play, I would go to that cabinet under the bar and grab a bottle of liquor. I wouldn't drink too much, but I know even then it was never just one drink. Again, that carefree, airy lightness would come over me. I would blast my dad's music on his stereo system—Pink Floyd, Led Zeppelin, The Doors. Sometimes I'd run up the stairs and take my brother's CDs—The Beastie Boys, 2Pac, The Offspring, and my own personal favorite: No Doubt's *Tragic Kingdom*. I loved music and dancing.

Those were some healthy forms I utilized to escape from myself. When I mixed all these together it made a most enjoyable cocktail. I'd dance and twirl and sing. I'd imagine I was on a stage performing in front of a large adoring crowd. Again, I had that feeling of contentment and freedom. Then someone would come home and my flight of fantasy would disappear. I would steal away to my bedroom where I spent the majority of my time, alone.

The first time I got completely drunk was on a trip with my friend to Big Bear, CA. It was wintertime, so I was excited to see snow. I hadn't seen snow since I had moved away from Utah. We stayed at her older sister's house. She was twenty-seven, and we were thirteen. She was fun, beautiful, and there was something mystical about her. When we first arrived, we put our bags in our room and came back downstairs. It was a beautiful cabin in the middle of the woods.

We sat on the couch and she brought over two large glasses of red wine. As she placed the glass in front of me she stated, "You know, red wine is really good for your heart. Drink some." So, I did. I drank the whole glass. That floaty, fun, carefree feeling hit me in all the right places. We talked about life, and I was entranced because she knew way more about everything than I did. She was extremely intuitive, so I naturally felt drawn to her. She had so much knowledge about astrology, something I started studying when I was ten. She seemed otherworldly, but I felt a fuzziness and a darkness surrounded her.

The atmosphere was light and cozy. Warm compared to the freezing temperatures just outside. My friend's sister decided to run to the store and pick up some food for dinner, along with some liquor. I was ecstatic. The red wine had started to wear off and I was ready to have a good time. When she got back she started preparing dinner and making cocktails. She brought us large cups filled with something that had a light greenish tint to it.

MOMMY DRUNKEST

There was salt around the rim of the glass. I asked, "What is this?" as she handed it to me. She exclaimed, "A margarita! Try it!" So I did. I liked it, kind of a weird aftertaste, but that didn't keep me from drinking that one, or the next five margaritas I asked for.

I was having a wonderful time, not a care in the world. We danced around the house, giggling and singing. I'm not even sure if we ended up eating the food her sister made. I felt like I was in another dimension where there was no time, no bad thoughts, no memories creeping around the corner to jump out and scare the lightness away. No actual thoughts about anything. I felt great. At some point the world started to spin a little. I would look at the wall and move my eyes from left to right and everything would slowly follow after, just trailing behind. I kept moving my eyes, because I couldn't believe what was happening. It was so strange, but I liked it.

We went back to our room. We kept laughing and talking about stuff that thirteen-year-old girls talk about, but much more candidly. I started getting a little too comfortable. I was dancing and I pulled my top off over my head, spun it around in the air, and flung it to the corner of the room. We were laughing and giggling the entire time. My friend did the same. I could never leave well enough alone, so off came my bra. I was totally freed of my self-consciousness and insecurity. I guess that country song is right; tequila really does make your clothes come off.

My friend and I weren't alone in that room. Her niece, who was about eight at the time, was in there just wanting to hang out with us older girls. Years later we would smoke that same girl out for the very first time. We were wonderful role models. When I woke up in the morning, I bolted out of bed, ran into the bathroom, and threw up in the sink. I stayed in front of that sink for at least forty-five minutes.

I looked in the mirror as I stood there. I was totally sick and totally miserable, wondering how the hell one can go from complete happiness, to sleep, to waking up feeling like they are going to die. I didn't eat, and I could feel my stomach eating itself, (which wasn't completely unusual for me), but this feeling I had never experienced before. My head was pounding and I was so nauseated. It was the worst I had ever felt in my entire life. This was my first hangover. As I was standing at the sink, looking in the mirror, flashbacks from the night before kept coming back to me. Nothing really bothered me, except the strip tease. I was mortified and couldn't believe I had done that. I swore to myself that I would not get this drunk or do anything like that again. This was the first time I told myself that, lying through my teeth and not even realizing it. I truly believed the lie. Those were the firsts of many, many, many, more to come.

… BRITTANY PRIESTLEY

Dilemma

Just another disappointment
There's no telling where it all went
The motives are twisted and bent
There's no telling what it all meant
Did reality ever play a part
Or was it a selfish mind fooling a tainted heart
Why does it always end before it starts
When will I learn to pull illusion and reality apart

CHAPTER EIGHT

Drug

I MET A GUY AT A bar. The first time I met him, I knew we would get married. He didn't remember our first meeting; he had too much to drink. A couple days later he approached me at that same bar. We played cat and mouse for a few months. I was twenty-one and I was a party girl. I had no interest in anything serious.

I had been badly burned by love, and all of my would be romances only lasted one night. I used men the way they had used me. I already acquired full blown alcoholism and I was having a passionate love affair with cocaine. I didn't give two shits about most things, especially life. I had suicidal thoughts for years, but it was at this time that my need for it to all end became most desperate.

Jack was the guy I met at the bar. He was perfect, because he was always ready to party. He didn't complain or harp on me about my drinking and love for cocaine. He happily joined in my sordid love affairs. I fell fast for Jack. He came into my life when I needed to be rescued. I didn't understand that no one could save me from myself. We had become inseparable. We had been dating three months when I decided to follow Jack, as he fled from California to Missouri. I thought I could escape cocaine, control my drinking successfully, and have my suicidal ideologies lifted, by uprooting and leaving everything behind.

I worked as a tables game dealer at a casino in the town where we lived. It was known as "The Boat" because it was built right along the Missouri River. I worked at the casino for five years. During my time there, I had my first two children. I quit drinking when I found out I was pregnant with my first child at eight weeks along, but not without a few more celebratory mimosas.

BRITTANY PRIESTLEY

After I gave birth to my beautiful daughter Astrid Jean, Jack brought me some champagne to celebrate one of the happiest days of my life. I was also given Vicodin, for pain, after the delivery. I was feeling high on this new feeling of maternal love, alcohol, and drugs. One doctor came in, and having no idea that I was an alcoholic, proceeded to tell me that darker beers, like Guinness, would help my breast milk come in faster. What!? That was the perfect tidbit of information for me to hear. I was told I should drink for a beneficial purpose, by a doctor. I sent Jack out to get me some Guinness right away.

Needless to say, I did not limit my alcohol intake to just that Irish beer. I tried to control how much I consumed. I'd give myself a twelve pack limit per night. Sometimes I stuck by that, usually not. On my days off from work, I would go full throttle. I would spend the day with my baby and drink. At this particular time I decided vodka and Peach Snapple sounded like a nice fit. My plan was to drink it more slowly, because it looked so nice in a chilled glass. It also tasted delicious and was so sophisticated. As it turns out, I did not drink them more slowly. Those were the lies I came up with to hide my alcoholism from myself.

MOMMY DRUNKEST

I still breastfed at this time. I would try to pump and dump, so the alcohol wouldn't contaminate my milk. Sometimes I would not. I would feed her formula when I had way too much to drink. Sometimes I would not. Eventually my breast milk dried up and I wasn't able to breastfeed her as long as I wanted to. I was a failure. I couldn't even put down the bottle long enough to give my baby the best and most natural nourishment I could provide.

During this time, I met a girl at work. She was blonde, tiny, and had a sadness about her. I will call her Hedy. Right off the bat she gave me a strange feeling. She was a cocktail server on the casino floor and we would chat when she came over to serve my tables.

Rather quickly, Hedy would disclose very personal and kind of horrifying stories about her life, mostly pertaining to her husband. I didn't find this too unusual, as people would often confide all kinds of things about themselves without even knowing me. She came to work one day with two black eyes and a broken nose. I knew it had been the handiwork of her husband. He was heavy into drugs, particularly meth.

There was one time I was using the ladies'

room at work. I heard the door open and footsteps coming down the corridor along the stalls. When I opened the door, Hedy was right outside of my stall. I almost knocked right into her. She gave me this creepy half smile, and I told her she scared me. She said, "I know." *Single White Female* flashed through my mind. Even though I had all these negative feelings about her, I still agreed to hang out with her outside of work. I felt bad for her.

She came to my house one evening. I had already started drinking my vodka with a splash of Peach Snapple. I was buzzed. We hung out and talked for a while. We played with baby Astrid. When I went to put my baby back in her Pack 'N Play to sleep or play with her toys, I dropped her. It wasn't a far fall, but it was enough to make her cry. I just thought, "Shit, Britt, you are drunk." I felt horrible.

When I came back Hedy got up to go to the bathroom and was in there for quite a while. When she finally did come back out, I had to use the bathroom. I didn't find anything out of the ordinary in there, but as I left the bathroom and walked down the hall, I saw her hovering over my drink. When she saw me she moved away from it quickly.

MOMMY DRUNKEST

We continued drinking and I started to feel really messed up, more than just drunk. She brought up the subject of cocaine and how we should get some. At this point, I hadn't done cocaine in almost two years. It sounded like a wonderful idea. I knew someone I could get it from and I made the phone call.

My husband overheard us from the other room and got really angry. When he and I had first met we did a lot of blow together, but that had been a couple of years before. Hedy started getting mouthy and really aggressive with him. I just sat there watching, trying to calm the situation down. Before I knew what was happening, he had grabbed us both by the arms and pushed us outside, with our purses flying behind. He locked the door.

At this point, I just wanted another drink. We got in her maroon Trans Am and drove to a bar down on Main Street. We sat at the bar and ordered our drinks. There were two guys sitting beside us. She looked over at them and then she looked at me and whispered, "We can have them buy our drinks and then go home and sleep with them." Immediately I said, "No, I can get my own." I was a little horrified, because I knew she was serious. That tingly feeling came back. It crept up my spine and into my neck telling me to go home and get away from her, but I just finished my drink and ordered another.

As we continued sitting at the bar, she started to act crazier by the minute. I started acting crazy too. I felt toasted. I knew it had to be more than just alcohol. The bar owner wanted us out. He knew me, of course, because I was a bar fly. For this reason, instead of calling the police, he called us a cab.

We got in the cab when it arrived, and I knew the cab driver as well. I slurred a greeting. We made small talk. Then he asked where we were going. I started to say home, but Hedy cut me off and started reciting her address. As we drove along I started to say home again, but she repeatedly said no, we were going to her house. At this point, I started to panic.

The whole night she had been flirty with me, and she had actually grabbed my face and kissed me on the lips at one point. I threw it under the rug, and just assumed she had too much to drink. She was saying a lot of sexual things and implying she wanted me in that way. I knew she wanted to take me home. She wanted to take me home to her husband. I yelled again, "I WANT TO GO HOME!"

MOMMY DRUNKEST

As the driver passed my street, I got out of my seat and punched the back of his head, so hard he screeched to a stop. He did not take me home. He stopped in front of the police station and literally threw us out of the back seat of his van. I hit the concrete hard, on my elbows and my knees. As I looked up from my fall, I saw Hedy flying down the street, running away from the police station as fast as she possibly could.

I was taken into the police station and put in a room with a female officer. I know I talked shit to her. I have this uncanny ability to pinpoint the very things people are most sensitive to; knowing what will hurt them the most. I did this most often when I was inebriated. I also have the ability to say what people need to hear most, but I was not looking to help this officer.

I was looking to hurt her. I must have gotten it right, because she slammed my head against the brick wall a few times. I don't remember what I said to her, but when Jack came to get me from the police station, with the baby and car seat in tow at three o'clock in the morning, she told him, "Your wife is a fucking bitch."

On the car ride home, I knew Jack was fuming.

I didn't blame him. He was yelling and cursing and saying, "Oh my God, if that was me I would've been thrown in jail! It is because of the way you look, you get away with everything!" Going on and on, and I was scared. When he pulled the car into our spot I knew what was coming next. He wasn't going to let me get away with anything.

He got out, and with the slamming of his car door, I jumped. He walked around the front of the car, threw my door open and ripped me out of the seat. I fell face down onto the gravel. He grabbed me by my hair, and he dragged me. He dragged me over the gravel. He dragged me over the wooden planks that bordered the grass. He dragged me over the torso-sized stepping stones, all fifteen of them, across the whole yard. He dragged me along the concrete. He dragged me over the metal door frame of the sliding glass doors, and he finally dragged me into the house and threw me into a heap on the linoleum floor. All the while I was screaming and kicking and thrashing, like a child throwing a tantrum. His grasp was too strong.

While I laid on that linoleum floor, I tried to forget the incredible pain in every inch of my body. As he was dragging me, every bone in my body had come into contact with every hard surface we passed. I tried to stop him, but with every resistance, there came an overpowering pull. I felt like the carcass of an animal that had just been hunted down.

All the while he told me I was a horrible mother, I was a bitch, I was a slut, a coke whore, shit for brains. Didn't he know I was already aware of all those things? I embodied all of those things and so many more. I was a horrible mother. What mother does this? What mother acts like this? Especially a new mother? I couldn't do anything right. Everyone knew it and I believed it. It was then I decided I would never try to obtain or snort cocaine again. I wouldn't do any other hard drugs again, either. I would stick to weed, pills, and booze and everything would be alright. Everything was going to be fine.

CHAPTER NINE

One Hundred Days

SHORTLY THEREAFTER I HAD MY second child, a bubbly sweet boy we named Noah Priestley. My husband and I started drinking, yet again. I had stopped drinking, for the second time, during my pregnancy. Jack did not. His drinking was actually at one of its worst points while I was carrying Noah. Our daughter, Astrid, was one-year-old at this time. He would drink whiskey and pick fights with me. We would argue as we always had. I think he only hit me once while I was pregnant, and I honestly can't even remember why.

MOMMY DRUNKEST

One night in February, he was really on a rampage and started yelling at me because he was hungry. He screamed that I never did anything for him, and I needed to make him food. He proceeded to throw food out of the refrigerator, slamming it to the floor. Glass was everywhere, food, broken eggs. He turned to me and told me to clean it up. I tried to stay out of his way, but it's hard to jump out of the way of a freight train when it's charging through your house.

I tried to shield Astrid from her father and his massive temper tantrum. I put her in my bedroom and played music for her to dance to. She was contented for a short while. Eventually, I went to the bedroom to put Astrid to sleep and hopefully to fall asleep myself, knowing full well that was not going to happen. He wouldn't let up. He wouldn't leave us be. It was impossible to steer clear of his anger when he got like this.

He kept yelling at me, telling me all the horrible things I already knew and hated about myself. He said I was a fat ass. I was pregnant, so I had gained weight. He always knew what to say to punch me in the gut. The thought came to my mind, that I've probably had a million times, "My daughter is going to think this is normal. She is going to think this is ok. I am showing her this is ok. This is the way a man is supposed to treat a woman that he loves." That scared the hell out of me. I would rather not get the police involved, but I was done with this tornado of a man ripping through our lives and my bedroom. I called the cops and had him put on a twelve hour hold.

Noah was born on a Sunday in the evening. Again, we had celebratory drinks. Again, I was given Vicodin. Jack was drunk when our son was born. I could tell, but I hoped no one else could. He cut the umbilical cord, as he did with all four of our children. Noah was placed in my arms. Instant deep love flooded every cell of my body, just like when I first held Astrid. I didn't know my heart had the capacity to love two children so wholeheartedly. He looked up at me with the sweetest eyes and I was joyously happy. I remained in that state of contentment for a while; the love for my new baby, the booze, and the pain killers were a magnificent elixir.

Seemingly out of nowhere, Jack stood up and declared, "I just had a son! I need to go out and celebrate with someone!" He left me at the hospital, with our newborn son, to go to a restaurant an old friend of his owned in Downtown Columbia. I felt deserted and so alone. My family was now living back in Utah, so they weren't with me. I wanted them to be, but my mom had planned to come out to help when I had to go back to work after maternity leave. I sat there so sad and so anxious. My only respite was my new baby.

A few hours later, I looked out the window of my hospital room and saw Jack trying to climb over the fence below. Insert massive eye roll here. I called him and told him to get away from the fence. Visiting hours were over, but I could still tell the nursing staff to let him in. I had to go out to the lobby to hold him up and steer him in the direction of my room. He had driven the car while he was wasted, and I had just given birth to his child. I was angry and so hurt. He handed me a bottle of whiskey. I smiled. He passed out.

It was April 22, 2012 and Noah was almost exactly one month old. I was still on maternity leave, so I was at home with the kids and I drank to fill my days, like I always did. I was also still on pain pills. I always called the doctor's office to get refills, saying I was still in pain even if I wasn't. Not physically anyway.

Jack was home on this particular day, and we started drinking together. He had been thinking about his grandfather, whom I never got the chance to meet. He had passed away before we met. Having a son really set something off in Jack. He had never met his biological father and had numerous step-fathers. His grandpa was the closest thing to a father he ever had. The more he morosely wandered down memory lane, the more he threw the drinks back. I'd been there myself a million times, just like every alcoholic or addict has. He grabbed the keys to my Honda CRV, which I had forgotten to hide on that particular day. He proceeded to walk out the sliding glass doors with the keys in his hand.

I had a feeling of dread, but I knew there was nothing I could do. If I did do something it might get physical and for some reason I remember thinking, "Let him go, this has to happen." I had to make an effort, even a small one, so I knocked on the glass. He turned to look at me with eyes that were not his own. They were a stranger's eyes, but I had come to know them well. Dark, mean, and absent. I looked straight into those eyes and said very calmly, "You will get a DUI if you go." He turned and walked away.

I was worried and thinking of all the worst case scenarios. When that happens I have to get rid of those thoughts immediately, so I continued to drink. I tried calling him several times, and was finally able to reach him. When I finally got through to him he had music blasting and said he was driving out in the corn fields. He rambled on about how he and his grandfather would go out there and he just wanted to be close to him. He hung up and I couldn't reach him for hours.

When I finally did see my CRV again, it was speeding down the street being followed by several police cars and a tan minivan with a family inside. He got arrested for DUI right in front of our house.

The next morning, Noah was scheduled to have a small procedure. A friend came with me. I wanted my husband to be there for this. I was a nervous wreck and he couldn't be there, he just wasn't there for us. He was sitting in jail. I told my friend I was done, and I meant it.

Jack and I started seeing a counselor for help with our marriage and substance abuse issues. We started occasionally attending 12-step meetings. In the town where we lived there is a recovery center, and we attended meetings with the patients there.

I remember hearing a woman speak about her children. She recounted that she didn't know how she got here, and that her kids were so angry with her. I felt her pain and I could never imagine myself putting my children through the same thing. I pitied her and thought I was not going to go down that road. I would not become the mother this woman had become.

I didn't know this at the time, but five years later I would be calling that exact treatment center home for thirty days. I decided I was going to do something different and get better. I wanted better, especially for my children. All I ever wanted was to protect them and nurture them.

I stopped drinking, because I knew Jack wouldn't stop if I didn't. I still thought he was the major problem, but it was only because he was the one spiraling out of control this time. I stood on my high horse and told myself at least I wasn't as bad as he was. Nonetheless, we both quit drinking. He attended the meetings more often than I did, because we both knew he needed it more. Life was nice. It was a relief to feel good; not hungover and groggy all the time.

MOMMY DRUNKEST

We went one hundred days without drinking any alcohol. We went one hundred days until he brought home a six-pack of Budweiser. I was hesitant, but it sounded good. At that point in my recovery, I was focusing all my energy on just not drinking. I wasn't doing anything else to change my life or my thought patterns. We could split this six-pack of beer and that would be all. That thought only lasted until they were gone and I was walking out the door to get more.

BRITTANY PRIESTLEY

MOMMY DRUNKEST

Love evoL

Happiness, Life, Truth, Trust
Destiny, Hate, Fucking Lust
Reject, Accept, Forgive, Forget
With All I Give, I Never Get Shit
We Must Hold, Keep, Seek, And Find
The Way, The Day, To Hold And Define
Smoke, Love, Want, Lust
There Is No One, Who Now, Holds Trust
Weak Mind, Small Heart
All Together We Fall Apart
Crime, Murder, Rape, Stealth
With All We Ask, We Never Get Help

BRITTANY PRIESTLEY

Breathe, Stop, Hold In, Kill

Stop, Breathe Out, Let Go, Feel

Hurt, Pain, And All The Mistrust

My Love Is Often Confused With Lust

Depend, Follow, Fall Behind

Lead, Seek, Keep, And Find

Fucked Up Ways, A Dirty Haze

Smiles Will Come, Maybe These Memories Will Fade

No One Will Ever Appreciate

Happiness, Life, Truth, Or Trust

It's All A Game

So Play We Must

MOMMY DRUNKEST

CHAPTER TEN

The Mortician's House

WHEN JACK AND I FIRST moved from California to Missouri, we lived with a roommate. Craziness ensued in that house, and it can all be traced back to liquor. We had a falling out with our roommate and needed to move out of that house before our new place was going to be ready. At the time, some of Jack's relatives lived nearby, so we stayed at their house for about a week in between rentals.

The house gave me the creeps. There was a lot of energy in that house, and some of it was dark. We stayed down in the basement. I did not like that basement. It was eerie and I always got the feeling I wasn't alone, even when I was. I had the feeling that someone or something was watching me. I could not sleep; I couldn't even pass out after having too many rounds at the bar. I decided I needed to take NyQuil. I took it every night we stayed there.

There were a few times I still awoke, and I'd lay there trying to avoid the malignant blackness that crept around, like that old friend that keeps showing up at your door after you've turned him away a million times. It was always around three o'clock in the morning. I asked if anyone else felt uneasy or strange in the house. I got nods, and I was told a man who happened to be a mortician had the house built and it doubled as his place of business.

Fast forward three years and now Jack and I had two children. We were given an offer to move into the morticians' house, no rent due for the first few months and Jack would do some remodeling and fix up the house a bit. One of the requirements was no alcohol. I had my reservations, because I knew how that house made me feel and something dwelled there that didn't belong.

The house did have more room for us though, and we were in a tight spot financially. As the saying goes, "Desperate times call for desperate measures." With all my reluctance and doubts in tow, we moved in and started fixing things up. I mainly picked out paint colors for the walls and cleaned. Jack did most of the work.

We were not supposed to drink. When I made that promise, I usually meant it. Deep down all that really meant to me was I just had to hide it better and maintain some sort of composure. However, there was no hiding it with me. If you couldn't smell it seeping from my pores, it was written all over my face. There was no maintaining anything, especially not my composure. The only thing I could truly maintain was my high from pot or pills and my ability to hunt down another drink. I couldn't not drink on a regular day. The house made me want to escape, not deal.

I did try. It was during this time that I sought the help of a physician for my drinking for the first time. I was prescribed naltrexone, which is supposed to curb the craving for alcohol. All it ever really did was increase the amount I needed to consume to get the desired effect. Pills always gave alcohol a little extra boost, and so I enjoyed mixing them together.

The basement had a large wash basin and a drain in the middle of the floor, for draining of bodily fluids. The cellar was a room on one side of the basement, and it was always freezing. We kept canned goods and water jugs in there, but it had previously housed dead bodies laying in wait. I tried to avoid the basement as much as I could, but I felt pulled to go down there all the time. There was an elongated garage attached to the basement, which had once been custom built for a hearse.

Beginning in the backyard, there was a pathway that led to the cemetery. I felt compelled to go to the cemetery, too. I drank more to stop the pulling, to stop the sensing, the feeling, everything. I didn't want to see what I saw or know what I knew concerning anything in that house. Jack just thought I was crazy. He rarely, if ever believed me.

The darkness had started to get to me and I knew it was seeping into Jack as well. We had dealt with issues involving various forms of abuse in our relationship. Not just him, not just me, but both of us. The abuse here got scary and severe. I had a black eye or some sort of bruise on my face, and bruises all over my body at all times. Some of my injuries were due to my drunken clumsiness and some were not.

I tried my best to hide my bruises with makeup,

but sometimes there just was no hiding it. I would be embarrassed to see people, but I still had to show up to work at the casino. I would make up the same kind of stories women tell when these things happen. I did it even though I knew people saw right through my lies and excuses, and straight into my broken spirit. I felt weak and pitiful. I felt helpless, stupid, and placed all the blame on myself.

I know that not to be true today. I did play a part in it, and I take full accountability for the part in which I played. I do not condone any man hitting any woman and vice versa, not in anger. I had learned that these things were normal, that violence and arguing where what happened in a relationship. I watched my parents.

When I was little and I would fantasize about my husband, in my fantasy we would argue and fight. Then we would make up. Now, with my real husband, I began to fight back. I hit, scratched, clawed, kicked, slapped, punched. I kicked him in the face and broke one of his back molars once while he was attacking me. There was only so much I could endure before I started to become the monster I feared. I retaliated and I also instigated. I knew how to push buttons and I did so intentionally.

MOMMY DRUNKEST

I wanted a reaction, I wanted friction. I felt that proved his love for me. If he didn't react, he didn't care, and if he didn't care then he didn't love me.

There was one incident that was so painful and my entire face was black and blue, and swollen. I could not move for days. I could not lift up my arms. I laid on the couch and I watched my kids play. Every time they walked or crawled over, and looked up at me with their sweet eyes, a part of me wanted to die. Their looks of confusion when they saw my battered and swollen face made me feel such a deep sense of self-loathing. I was letting this happen. I was letting them see me like this, and I didn't know what to do or how to make it stop.

I drank. I drank to forget. I drank to numb the pain, both physically and spiritually. I couldn't face reality. I couldn't accept that I was being abused by a man I loved. I couldn't fathom why I wanted it to happen and why I felt that I deserved to be punished. I didn't know why I always had to be a victim. I didn't see how well I played that part. I hoped I could forget, knowing damn well I could not. I prayed my children could forget seeing me like this. I prayed they wouldn't remember and they wouldn't become damaged. I didn't want them to be like me. The only thing I ever wanted was to protect them and love them unconditionally. But I couldn't protect them. I couldn't do anything right. I was told I was worthless, and I believed it. Out of all the names I had been called, that one broke my heart the most.

Jack and I played these stupid intoxicated toxic games. Games all about control. We would hide the liquor, pills, or weed from each other. We would take money, debit cards, and car keys away from each other. It was infuriating. It was tumultuous. We also took turns locking each other out of the house.

On one particular day, it was him locking me out of our house. It was freezing outside that day. I was insanely livid and incredibly drunk. I was overcome with so much anger, anger that felt as if it were coming from the outside in. I ran around the house, checking for unlocked doors and windows, any way in, and I found none. I screamed for him to let me in. He refused. I ran down the steps to the driveway and stopped in front of the garage door that had once housed a hearse. Three windows ran along the top of the garage door.

I stood in front of one window, catching my own reflection in it and just stared for a minute. I heard,

"Do it." I remember thinking I definitely should not. I felt overcome and I punched my right hand through that window, shattering the glass. I ripped it back out. Blood, blood everywhere. I was shocked and I ran back up the steps to the front door, trailing blood behind me. I screamed for him to open the door, and he must have heard the panic in my voice, because the door opened.

A look of complete shock came over his face as he first looked around and then focused on me. The entire front porch and steps looked like a murder scene. For some reason that day Jack did not drink. Thank God. He rushed to grab me a towel that I wrapped around my arm. It became instantly saturated with my blood. He got our two-and-a-half-year-old daughter and not yet one-year-old son out of the house, into the car, and strapped into their car seats. I climbed into the car and remained silent until we arrived at the hospital.

In the emergency room they began stitching me up. I had a deep gash in the middle of my lower right arm. I could see the fatty tissue pushing its way out from underneath my skin. There were several other cuts all around the big gash. The police had arrived for questioning right after Jack left with the children.

I was thankful he took them away. They didn't need to be there, seeing me this way. They didn't deserve any of what I was putting them through.

The police officer had passed Jack on his way out, and being familiar with our history, was prepared to arrest him. The police officer was convinced Jack had done something to me to land me in the ER, but when that police officer came into the exam room, he finally saw me for what I was. I was not a completely innocent battered wife. He saw my volatile, mean side that was completely out of control. He saw past the role I had to play to save my own ass when the police showed up at my house, which was often. Jack was not innocent either, but I sure did throw him under the bus in order to maintain the facade I needed others to believe.

When the cop left and the doctor came back into the room he looked at me quite seriously and said, "You know, you are very lucky. If you had been cut a couple centimeters either up or down on your arm you would've hit a major artery. You would have bled out. You could have died." I thought, "What a way to go." The kids would say, "I don't really remember my mom, but she was a drunk who accidentally killed herself breaking a window."

What a wonderful legacy I would leave behind for my children. I had spent a good portion of my life wanting to die, but now that I had that image in my mind, I didn't want to leave my children behind. I couldn't leave them. I had to make a change. Not a change in me, that would be too hard and I wasn't yet ready to face myself. I needed a change in scenery. I wanted to be closer to my parents.

We lived in the mortician's house for only four months, but what a four months that was. The darkness I felt in that house seemed to attach itself to me, and my excessive drinking to block the bad energy there was not working. It only intensified everything and made a cozier breeding ground for the darkness to grow. Jack had been arrested several times while we lived in that house. I was arrested and put in jail for the first time in my life. I was malnourished, beaten, and bruised. It was not just physically, but in every way possible. There was so much negativity. If I just left and got as far away from that house and that town as possible, then everything would get better. It had occurred to me to stop drinking, but I knew that wasn't going to happen. I wasn't ready to let it go. Not yet.

CHAPTER ELEVEN

No Smoking Allowed

I LEFT MISSOURI BEHIND WITH my two small children, and not much else. My sister-in-law flew to Kansas City to meet up with us and help with the drive back to Utah. For that I have always been grateful. I didn't go without liquor in tow. I made sure to buy some whiskey on my way to the airport. I thought I'd get a chance to drink it, but I ended up driving the majority of the trip. Very smart on her part.

I was excited to get away from everything I was leaving behind, the darkness and the mess. I was happy that I could be near my family again, so they could have a close relationship with my children. I was not too ecstatic to be living with my parents again at twenty-seven, but I believed it would only be temporary until Jack and I could get our lives together. Jack stayed behind to deal with some legal issues. I had some to deal with as well, but I would handle it from Utah and I did.

The first night in Utah we all went to eat at In-N-Out Burger. I had missed that food so much. It had been at least four years since I last tasted it. I was happy to be with my parents. When we got back home, I went to the bathroom and threw up all the food I had just eaten. I then proceeded to spend the rest of the night with Jack Daniels.

The only thing I changed at that time was my address. I didn't change anything about myself. I didn't change my mind set or make any promises to be better to myself. If anything, my drinking picked up momentum quickly. I tried hiding it, like I always did. Hiding all of the destructive behaviors I had come to find comfort and solace in. There was no trying to fight it. I knew I wouldn't win.

I hid bottles and beer cans under beds, under mattresses, in drawers, out in the bushes, in coat pockets. This was something I always did for as long as I can remember. I became so good at hiding whatever liquor and drugs I had that I often hid them from myself, which really pissed me off. I'd disguise it with mouthwash, lotion, perfume, gum, and distance. I would not get close to anyone. When I think about this today it sounds completely insane, but it also makes me sad. I regret not hugging and kissing my parents more. Feeling like I couldn't. Really I was just choosing my love of alcohol over the love I had for my parents.

I was disappointed that life had brought me to this point. I missed Jack. I worried about him, because I knew he missed us and he wallowed in the bottle. When my money would run out and I had none to buy alcohol, I would take my mom's wine. She had a whole crate of it in the garage that she had forgotten was there. When she found out what I had been doing she gave it all away. That made me angry. Didn't she realize that if she just let me have them I wouldn't be so hostile? Didn't people realize that if they just gave me what I wanted, especially concerning alcohol, everything would be peaceful? Jack sent me some money, but when that ran out I would ask my mom, and if her answer was no, I'd take it anyway.

I'd make up lies about where I needed to go and use the kids as an excuse, just so I could venture out to the liquor store. In Utah, only beer is sold at gas stations and grocery stores. One more than one occasion, several actually, I would be in the parking lot of the liquor store counting down the minutes before the doors opened at 11:00 a.m. Other people would be waiting for the doors to open as well. Several times I remember thinking, "Oh my, I have become one of those people." Honestly, I had been of those people for a long time. All the sneaking and hiding forced me focus my time and attention around the liquor, even more than I had before.

Being around my parents made old forgotten memories resurface. They still treated each other the way the always had, not well. I became angry and even more resentful towards them. I began to see how their fighting had affected me. Now my kids would see it too. I didn't want my kids to be subject to the same thing I had been subjected to as a child. Insane thinking on my part, considering how much Jack and I had put them through and the chaos they had to live with in our home.

My Honda CRV got repossessed. That was

mortifying. I had always been responsible when it came to making payments. That was just one more thing that made me feel like a complete failure. I felt like my freedom was taken away from me. I'd have to borrow my dad's truck and I'd sometimes drive it drunk to go buy more alcohol. I really hated to do that, not because of the recklessness and irresponsibility, but more because I didn't want to get caught. I had never gotten a DUI, and I still haven't. Not yet.

My mom's lifelong friend, who had been our neighbor when we lived in Utah years before, would come by the house. She had been one of the women who would sit around the table drinking wine. She gave me a memoir of a woman who was an alcoholic to read. We talked about life and what I had been going through. She told me to call her anytime I needed something.

I was not one to accept help willingly. I had learned that self-sufficiency was best and I needed to handle my problems on my own. By handle, I meant bury. Burying, masking, escaping, numbing my problems—that was how I handled most things. I found that once I opened my eyes, they were all still right there smacking me in the face and worse than ever.

One day I was drinking and took some prescription pills that were not mine. I was way out there. I knew I had crossed the line with my consumption that day. I tried to control it, because I was home alone with the kids. Usually it was ok and we would have dance parties and play, but today was different. I called my mom's friend and asked her to come by. I needed help. Thank God she was able to at that moment. She came over and found me passed out on the bathroom floor with two kids playing in the tub.

That was scary, but hadn't I been responsible by calling someone to come take care of my kids? Now I'd done it. Now I was going to have to deal with the lectures and the whole, "You need help" routine. The whole "Why can't you just stop, Brittany?" never-ending saga. Immediately my parents began looking into rehab facilities and places to detox. I fought with them about that for awhile. I told them I couldn't leave the kids behind. In response to that, they found a detox center where I could bring my children.

I called Jack to discuss it with him, and he convinced me that I should go. What had happened was unacceptable and I agreed. That didn't mean I wanted to go, and I made sure to get good and drunk before my mom took us. That was a bad idea. Alcohol tended to make me angry, and I'm an alcoholic, so I will continue to want a drink until I pass out. I was pissed that people were making me do this. On top of that, I wasn't allowed to have my phone and I wasn't allowed to smoke cigarettes at this detox center. Upon hearing that, I managed to grab a full pack of Marlboro Red 100's and put them in my underwear. They were not taking my cigarettes.

As my mom was filling out registration paperwork at the front desk, I sat there on a bench with my belongings and my children, just stewing. A woman walked down the corridor and started talking to me. I thought she was a little off her rocker and I wanted absolutely nothing to do with her. She told me this was her third time here coming off meth, and that I would like it here. Yeah, fucking right I would. I would be stuck in here with the likes of her? I wasn't a meth head, for crying out loud. I wasn't like any of these people. I was better, I was smarter. I could figure this out on my own.

My mom finished up with the receptionist. They

walked towards us together. My mom looked reluctant, because she knew how I could get when I drank. They said I was all set. I already wanted another drink and a damn cigarette. I resigned, and with the kids, followed the receptionist to our room. It was a small room with windows that could not be opened, looking out to some grass. Just perfect, how the hell am I supposed to smoke in here!?

She walked us to the dining area to get something to eat. I sat there with my kids, helping them eat. I panicked and instantly knew I couldn't do this. I can't be here with my kids. I can't be here, period. I got up and marched over to the receptionist and told her I needed to make a phone call. She didn't want to let me, but I was determined, and I scared her enough that she finally relented. I called my mom and demanded that she come and get me. She argued, but I did what I did best; I manipulated and made her feel guilty for all the things I always made her feel guilty about when I wanted something from her. I knew what to say in order to get her to fold and for me to come out with the winning hand.

I told the receptionist to give me back my things, and I gathered the rest of my possessions from the room. That poor lady tried to convince me to wait in the building for my mother, but I had to get out of that building. I was suffocating. I would not be held hostage. I walked as far away as I could and found some grass to sit on underneath a tree. I sat there with my two small children and our luggage as cars passed by wondering what we were doing. I was just waiting for my mom to come save me from this nightmare.

When she finally got there, I promised I'd be better and that I would attend 12-step meetings. I had been going to them since I was eighteen, always drunk and never listening to a damn thing. It always seemed to calm my mother down when I said I'd go. I meant it at that point. I was willing to do and say anything just to get back home. I said I'd work harder to slow down or even stop; knowing all I really meant was I had to do a better job at hiding it and not getting so wasted that I passed out in the middle of the day. I would start later in the day, stop with the hard liquor, try to eat before I drank, try to eat period, try not to throw up after I ate. All the same experiments I had already tried, over and over again. This time I would work harder and things would get better, but from past experience I knew things would only get worse.

MOMMY DRUNKEST

"I can't explain myself, I'm afraid, Sir, because I'm not myself you see."
    -Alice Liddell

CHAPTER TWELVE

Mommy Drunkest

I AM GOING TO TAKE a moment to say a few things before I begin with this part of my life. I strongly believe that drugs and alcohol bring out the absolute worst in people, especially when it's abused. I know this from extensive research, and I played the role of the more than willing guinea pig. I believe the energy surrounding it is evil.

The word "alcohol" is said to come from the Arabic term, "Al-Khul" which means, "Body-Eating Spirit". That speaks volumes to me. It devours so much more than just the body. It can and will devour everything and anything as long as you will allow it to, and I did just that.

When I drank, it was as if my spirit or my soul was snatched up and replaced by a completely foreign evil entity. My personality, my demeanor, my eyes all took on a different guise, completely concealing any part of me that was true and real. Several people made comments about this disturbing switch—I looked possessed, evil, scary. My own mother would be terrified and she would look into my eyes and say, "You are the devil."

It seemed my whole life I had been followed by darkness. I sensed Satan wanted me, and every time I drank I gave him an open invitation to be in my life. It had not always been to that extreme. I would have fun at times, but even when it was still fun, in an instant it could switch. I had absolutely no control over what emotion was going to come barreling to the surface and could take no action to stop it. I was a party girl.

When I lived in California, my friends and I used to go to Cabo San Lucas and Cancun. We lived three hours from the Mexican border, where the legal drinking age is eighteen. It was a four hour drive to Las Vegas from Southern California, so we also made that trip several times a year.

At first alcohol and drugs made me do things I never thought I could do; open up, tell my secrets, be less shy, feel comfortable in my own skin. Then there came a point where drugs and alcohol made me do things I never dreamed in my wildest nightmares I would do.

I am not disclosing any of this to pass the blame, or say that the devil made me do anything. I am simply stating that this disease, sickness—whatever you want to call it—knows no bounds. It controlled my life and I was but a slave sitting on the passenger side, helplessly watching it all unfold. During my time as an addict, I was good at deceiving others, but the person I deceived most was myself.

What I am about to say is something excruciatingly painful for a mother to admit. It is a sick secret we like to keep to ourselves, because of the immense shame it causes. I know now that I am not the only one with this secret. It wasn't until I got sober and had conversations with other mothers that I realized I was not alone. I felt what I had done was unforgivable. I thought no one, but myself, could ever be sick and demented enough to do it.

MOMMY DRUNKEST

Out of all the terrible, mean-spirited, hurtful things I had done during my years of inebriation, none compared to this: I drank and got drunk during my last two pregnancies.

In a million years, I never thought I would admit this to another human being. My plan was to take it to the grave. I wouldn't even admit it to the people in my life who knew I was doing it at the time. I denied it every time. For a long time, I wouldn't even be able to admit it to myself. I buried it deep and then I drowned it with more liquor. The shame and guilt were soul crushing, and it ate at me all the time.

There are no words to describe the repulsion I felt towards myself and my actions. I don't think I ever truly loved myself, and most of the time I'm pretty sure I hated myself. After this, I knew I truly despised myself. I could not stop. I wanted to with all my heart, and I just couldn't. I believed that if I didn't drink it would cause more harm than good. I was afraid of quitting cold turkey and withdrawing. I was scared my body would go into a state of shock and the baby and I would both be worse off. I did really try to keep my consumption to a minimum, but sometimes I couldn't.

What had been a joyous time with my first two

pregnancies was not with these two. I was still living with my parents and Jack had made the move to Utah to be with us. I had my family around me, just like I had wanted so badly with my first two pregnancies. I should have been elated and grateful. I had moments of happiness, because I knew I already loved these babies, but I was tortured knowing that my love, a mother's love, the strongest love there is, wasn't enough.

That stark realization was hard to fathom. It should have been enough. I had a difficult time accepting that. There was something definitely wrong with me. I was a shitty, selfish, horrible mother. What kind of mother could do this? I never thought it would be me.

Looking back on my life, I started to notice how every time I said I would never do something or thought that something could never happen to me, it was like the universe started setting that very thing into motion. Call it a coincidence, call it a lesson in humility, call it what you want. I have learned never to think that there is anything out there that can't happen to me. But for the grace of God, there go I.

I prayed continuously during my last two pregnancies. All day and all night. I had never prayed as much before that point, and I'm not sure I have since. I prayed that the babies would be well and healthy. Over and over again, I would say, "God, please let this baby be ok. Please let this baby be ok." The fear and terror of what I had possibly done to my unborn children was too much.

Sometimes I felt like I couldn't breathe. It was a dark time. I had wanted to die during several years of my life, but this was different. I never wanted to die and live so much at the same time. I would lay awake all night sometimes, with my brain, stuck in a continuous pattern of thoughts, just reeling. My mind would take me down dark avenues and into inescapable trenches, filled with all the possibilities of what was sure to go wrong. The darkness was so thick and consuming that my prayers and pleas couldn't break through. Those nights were the worst, most lonely nights of my life.

I was in such a state of complete denial, that when I started to feel contractions, I was convinced they were Braxton-Hicks contractions. Those contractions aren't the real deal. I decided to get into the shower and by the time I was washed and ready to get out, I could hardly stand. I kept telling myself, "This isn't happening. I'm not ready yet." I was terrified to see what damage I had caused my unborn baby. I was terrified of being a mother to three small children.

No matter how much I didn't want to go into labor, I was definitely going into labor. I was doubled over in excruciating pain. I couldn't even get my own pants on. I somehow managed to get to the car, with the help of Jack, who was completely beside himself. I got into the passenger side and held on for dear life. I kept yelling at him to get me to the hospital faster. We lived about ten minutes from there. I was pretty sure I was going to have my baby in the car. I tried my best to breathe and remain calm, but I was experiencing so much pressure and pain I didn't think it was actually possible.

I felt like my baby's head was going to burst out right then. Jack dropped me off in front of the hospital doors and I got to the elevator and repeatedly pressed the up button, hoping I wasn't going to deliver yet. I rushed down the hall as fast as I was able and ran up to the nurses' desk. I started to tell them I was about to give birth, but my water broke all over the floor before I could get my sentence out. I didn't even say anything; the look on my face said it all.

MOMMY DRUNKEST

It was like a scene from a movie. The nurses rushed me to a room and helped me take off my clothes and put on a gown. I had to start pushing right away. There was no waiting. I was told to push and the pain I felt was incredible. I felt like my vagina had been lit on fire and I screamed, "Fuck!" The nurse told me to shut up and push, so I did one last time. My son, Luke Ernest, was born just six minutes after getting to the hospital. He was healthy. He was lovely. I loved him instantly and thanked God for him. I didn't have any celebratory drinks after his birth.

Fast forward eleven months and my Grandma Joanne, my mom's mother who I loved and had a very strong connection with, passed away. We were kindred spirits. Right after her death, I became pregnant again. Of course, I was still drinking, and even more so, because my grandma had just died. Each year that passed my drinking worsened.

When I found out I was pregnant again, I couldn't believe my body was even capable of carrying another baby. I weighed ninety pounds, because life was out of control and I resorted to controlling it the best way I knew how. I kept drinking. I prayed and I prayed to God, and I begged for some sort of sign that everything was going to be alright.

A few nights later I had a dream. I call it a dream, but I had experienced this many times and I know it was more than that. It was real. I was standing in my bathroom. Out of nowhere, a face appeared and startled me. When I realized it was my Grandma Joanne, who had just passed away, I felt calm. I looked right at her and I asked her if everything was going to be alright. I asked her about the baby. She told me she had seen the baby and she would be fine. I did not know the gender of the baby at this time. I suspected I would be having another little girl, and this was confirmation for me. I opened my eyes and knew that I had just been visited by my dead grandmother.

I still drank. I still felt the same way I did when I drank with Luke, and this was just as bad, if not worse. I hadn't learned a damn thing. I still couldn't stop. With all the pain and agony I had put myself through the last time, here I was doing it again. Insanity. Total and complete insanity. Violet Rose was born healthy, sweet, and beautiful. Again, I didn't know a heart could hold so much love. I didn't deserve to be blessed with four beautiful children. I had no idea why God had given them to me.

All I knew was there were women out there who wanted children and couldn't have them. Women who wanted children they would never have, and I took all of my blessings for granted. I felt so much guilt. Why was it me who received these gifts and not a more worthy woman? God works in mysterious ways, or so I've been told. I believe we unearth the truth when we are ready to hear it.

I want to tell any mother out there who has gone through this, is going through anything like this, or who will go through this: You do not have to go through it alone. You do not have to let the guilt and shame eat you alive. The unconditional love and the desire I had to take care of my children couldn't stop the devil I had invited into my life with safe passage via a bottle.

Alcohol is not just a body-eating spirit. It also eats away at your mind, your relationships, and your self-respect. Drugs and alcohol have the power to kill in every way a person can be killed, without dying. Then, after it has killed off everything it can slice its hooves through, it will bring the end. The worst part is, by then you will be begging for it.

CHAPTER THIRTEEN

Getting Away With It

FOR AS LONG AS I can remember my dad would call my mom names, a less offensive one he used with regularity was enabler. When I was young I didn't understand the meaning, but I knew it was always spoken regarding my oldest brother. My mom did bail him out. She bailed him out of jail, she bailed him out when it came to money, and she bailed him out in lots of other ways over the years. I cannot say that someone else is an alcoholic or addict, with the exception of myself, but whenever drugs or alcohol were involved he seemed to get into trouble.

MOMMY DRUNKEST

I watched these transactions take place and quickly learned the true nature of enabling. I also knew that one day I would be able to take advantage of it myself. As I got older and started making bad decisions, I knew that my mom would do the same for me as she had done for my brother. The first time I remember her enabling my bad behavior was while I was in the seventh grade.

I had smoked weed with a friend who had written a letter about it to another friend. The school confiscated the letter and all involved parties were called to the principal's office. I was terrified. I never got into trouble at school. The school notified my mom. It was a Friday, and the following day was Halloween. I begged my mom not to tell my father, because if he knew the truth I was going to be in real trouble.

She did not tell him. I was still able to go out with my friends for Halloween, one of my favorite holidays, and we had a really good time. The school had not implemented any punishment either. I had gotten away with it. I began to think that I could get away with anything. The cover-ups and enabling would only get more serious as I got older.

When I was twenty years old I went to a music

festival in Indio, California known widely as Coachella. I partied hard, drinking and rolling on ecstasy. I was stranded there by my friend, who was supposed to be my ride home. My mom, dad, brother, sister-in-law, and family dog drove four hours to come get me. I spent the night with complete strangers. That same night, I had also gotten arrested for minor in possession and then released. I did get a ticket, but the court threw out the charge. The paperwork had been done incorrectly. I got away with that too.

My oldest brother had gotten several DUIs, and my mom would have done anything to keep me from following the same path. She would drive anywhere, at any time to take me to or pick me up from a party, a club, or a bar. Whenever I went out, I knew I wouldn't have to drive. I was given the green light to drink as much as I wanted, and I always did. She even bought me alcohol before I turned twenty-one. I believe she relented and bought it, because she knew if she did not, I would make her life a living hell.

I spent so much of my life believing the world and all its people owed me something, owed me everything I felt rightfully mine. My parents owed me for not protecting me when I was little. My mom owed me for working all the time, leaving me feeling abandoned. Somebody, probably God, owed me for not making me perfect.

The list could and did go on forever. I always felt something had been taken from me; my innocence, my trust, my value. There was a price to be paid for my pain. I was owed and if someone didn't want to give me what was mine, paid in full, I was going to take it. Of course, no one knew they were supposed to give me what I wanted and what I felt entitled to. These massive debts only existed in my mind and in my bottomless vault of a memory bank.

When I was living with my parents again, in my late twenties, with my husband and four small children, I felt ashamed. I was extremely unhappy and the depression naturally brought about an increased consumption of alcohol. I had a live-in babysitter. I knew if I crossed the line and got too wasted my mom would be there to take care of my kids, and pick up the pieces that I had smashed to the ground. Literally and figuratively. I was out of control. I knew my parents would do nothing about it. I knew their threats of kicking us out were empty.

Jack and I did put them through hell. All of them: my parents, their friends, my other family members, my children. The domestic violence picked up and worsened. Again, I would try to hide it, but I couldn't. My left eye got the worst of it. To this day scar tissue is still visible under that eye. Blood vessels were broken and blood filled the white of my eye.

When my oldest was in kindergarten, I would go to events at her school looking like that. Since I could not hide it physically, I tried to hide it from myself by getting drunk. I went to her kindergarten graduation wasted on whiskey. Luckily, I didn't cause a scene. I went with her to dance classes drunk. My mom would give us a ride. Her class wasn't until four in the afternoon, and I could very seldom wait that long.

At the classes I would talk to one of the other moms as we watched our girls learn to be ballerinas. I had an intense urge to tell her something I knew she would find strange. I never knew where these messages came from, and I usually kept them to myself, but I had been drinking. That always allowed me to care less about appearing completely crazy.

MOMMY DRUNKEST

I told her she needed to reach out to an older male in her family, probably an uncle, and it was important that she do it soon. She looked at me for a second and said, "Ok." The next week she rushed up to me, thanking me. She had spoken to her uncle who lived in Brazil. He had died a couple days later. She had gotten a final good bye. I was happy to have helped, but something that always concerned me was who I received these messages from. I hoped it was God. Entanglement with the devil had me concerned.

My daughter's dance recital came soon after. I drank before going and brought alcohol with me, running to the bathroom every chance I got to steal another gulp. My favorite way to disguise my alcohol was by putting vodka in a water bottle. No one suspected a thing, or so I thought. I did usually get away with deceiving people with that trick. Most people were so unsuspecting, because who brings liquor to these events? Who puts vodka in a water bottle? An alcoholic does.

I stole my father's prescription pills. I got away with that for a long time. He suspected my mother and I allowed her to take the blame. My parents already fought, picked at, and argued with each other enough as it was, but I was more than willing to add fuel to that fire as long as I could continue to take those pills without any consequence. I was only ever concerned with myself, and my own need to just feel ok. Always to the detriment of others.

The police were called to my parents' house more times than they ever had in their thirty-plus years of marriage, while Jack and I lived with them. I never once got in trouble, even though I was usually the culprit. I just knew when to keep my mouth shut, put on an air of innocence, and let them assume what they wanted. They never assumed it was me causing problems. Even though, more often than not, I was to blame. I would do just about anything to ensure that I wasn't arrested and taken to jail ever again, especially in front of my children.

My mom had slowly and carefully tried to pull back and not enable me as much. She would no longer take me to get more alcohol when I had already been drinking. I had to resort to driving drunk, because I had no other choice. I had to have more. I was usually pretty good about having a stock-pile and back-up stash for times like these, but one particular day, I must have miscalculated.

I snuck out and drove to the gas station to get

more beer. The liquor store was too far, and I had made that drive drunk a couple of times. My higher self about had a heart attack every time I did that, so I tried to avoid it when possible. I arrived at the gas station, went inside, grabbed what I needed, and walked back to my GMC Yukon. As I pulled out of my parking space, I felt a bump. I had backed into an older lady's car. It wasn't hard, but I panicked. I was drunk and I could not deal with cops at the scene of this accident.

I put the car back into drive and sped out of there as quickly as possible. All the while, a man was frantically waving his arms at me, chasing me, and attempting to get my license plate number. I sped all the way home, repeatedly saying, "Oh, shit. Oh, shit. Oh, shit." I sped into my driveway, glancing over at the broken fence I had run into a few days earlier while drunk. I rolled my eyes and wondered why the hell Jack hadn't fixed it yet, as always expecting him to fix the things I'd broken.

I put the SUV in park, took my seatbelt off, jumped out, grabbed my beer, and hightailed it into the house. I frantically looked for Jack, and when I found him I told him he needed to get the license plates off of my car immediately. I tried to explain, but I told him to just do it. It was urgent. The plan to keep myself anonymous fell through rather quickly. There was a knock on the front door. My dad yelled at me from upstairs that the police were here and wanted to speak with me. Shit.

For some reason, I told my dad to relay the message for them to meet me in the driveway and they did. I was working really hard to maintain my composure, trying to conceal any trace of inebriation. I already had a cigarette lit as I walked towards them. I was sure that they were taking me to jail. Once again, I would have to spend the night in a jail cell, away from my kids, and regretting my choices. Kind of funny how remorse usually didn't come into play until after I'd been caught. I obviously wasn't thinking about their welfare when my tunnel vision kicked in and all I could think about was reaching for another beer or another bottle.

The cops started asking me questions. I didn't deny anything, I didn't lie. One thing I had learned over the years is that cops hate liars. They kind of laughed about the license plates. Then they looked at me and laughed, and said, "You are pretty tipsy, aren't you?" Not really a question at all, because my attempt at appearing sober did not work.

My eyes, my demeanor, my eloquent slurring of words didn't conceal a damn thing. I admitted I had a few drinks. I was just standing there waiting for the handcuffs to come out. They told me the old lady I bumped into had no damage and did not want to press charges. They said they had not been there to witness the accident, so they weren't going to arrest me. They told me not to leave my house again that night. I could have been charged with a hit-and-run while under the influence, and nothing happened. I had gotten away with it. My dad, on the other hand, was told if they had to come back and see me again, he would be the one arrested.

Jack was relieved, but upset at the same time. He always noticed when I got away with something, and had to mention why I got away with everything. He would always say it was because I was a small, pretty, blonde, white girl. I guess an archetype for innocence and goodness. He always said if that had been him he would've been tased and taken away, no questions asked. Probably. Regardless, I didn't understand it. Getting away with things didn't do me any good, and I knew I was on borrowed time.

The last few months we lived in Utah were tumultuous. On Mother's Day that year, Jack had gotten mad about something and stormed out of the house. I assumed he fled to a bar we frequented, without me. I was pissed. I had been drinking too, and I decided I would go up there to make him come back home and spend the day with us. I drank and I plotted, planned and drank.

Finally, I made up my mind and drove to the bar. I was incredibly angry, and everyone in the place knew it. Not because of my face or the way I was walking, not by my voice. I was silent. For whatever reason I have always been able to have an effect on the energy of a room. When I was angry, everybody felt it, and the atmosphere would become uncomfortable. We were quickly asked to leave, not because we were fighting, but because I had been there a few days prior and seemed to have really pissed off a cocktail waitress. When he was asked to leave, Jack, intoxicated, refused. When the cops arrived, we both got tickets for disturbing the peace and walked home in the rain. He had already gotten into trouble with the law for a domestic disturbance a couple months before that.

When he went to court for it all in June of 2016, he had the book thrown at him, so to speak. The judge knew about his lengthy past with the law. The

Utah judge shouldn't have known about the offenses from a different state, but I knew exactly who had informed that judge, and it wasn't me. It was an act of malice, maybe backed by a tiny amount of good intention. Jack wasn't ready to deal with the repercussions of his actions, not to that degree. He wanted to escape. He started making plans to move our family back to Missouri.

BRITTANY PRIESTLEY

MOMMY DRUNKEST

"Now, here, you see, it takes all the running you can do, to keep in the same place."
　　　-The Queen of Hearts

CHAPTER FOURTEEN

Homeless

WHEN I HEARD JACK'S VERDICT come out of the judge's mouth, it entailed what he would be obligated to pay every month, the legal fees, and the length he would have to go to in order to stay on the right side of the law. All of this pertained to getting and remaining sober, and I knew exactly what his move was going to be. It was going to be a move far away from Utah. Far away from my family.

Everything in me screamed that I did not want to go. I did verbalize my feelings and strong resistance, but I knew that the damage had already been done. I was completely in denial of the situation at hand, even as my belongings were being packed away into boxes. I did not want to go, but I knew I couldn't stay. I felt utterly helpless to do anything about it. So I sat back, I watched, and I let it happen.

I drank and I drank and I drank, the entire time. I let so many things just happen when I drank. Almost like I was some nonparticipant observer, watching someone else's life happen. Life wasn't about living; life was something that just happened to me. I was completely detached from so many things: reality, my own life, myself. I had lost the power of choice. I sat back and tried ineffectively to escape my current situation. No matter how drunk I got my reality was sobering.

My oldest child was five, the next in line was four, the third was two, and my youngest was seven months old. My mom helped with the packing. Jack did most of the work and I helped reluctantly, mostly keeping the kids entertained and out of the way. We had two days to get as much done as possible. I said my goodbyes in tears. I knew I was going to miss them. I always did when I was away. I knew I would miss their support. I didn't have any friends in Missouri, not really good friends anyway. Any friendships I had were ruined because of my drinking.

We had no plan for where we would live when we got there. Plans like that don't happen during frantic packing over two days. Jack just wanted to get out as quickly as possible. Every mile we drove, I thought we could just turn around. Jack can just deal with this. I want to go back. Instead I asked him to stop at a gas station so I could buy some beer.

He never really liked Utah and complained about it often. For him, the best option for the family was to uproot us with no definitive plan. It's a terrible feeling to have no sense of security. We hauled our four small children, two dogs, a cat, a hamster, and a betta fish in our Yukon, with a trailer hitched to the back. Jack drove the entire trip, and I sat in the passenger seat watching the world fly by, sipping on my beer and holding on for dear life. My anxiety was at its highest point, just under the surface. We didn't stay overnight anywhere. Jack just drove straight through, getting nowhere fast.

When we made it to Missouri our first trial run was at a friend's house. He had been Jack's friend for many years. He was single with no children. I think it was definitely a shock to his system to have us all in his home. It didn't help that I drank and stole pills from his bathroom cabinet. I didn't and still don't know what they were, but I took them anyway. We had put all of our belongings in storage. I felt so lost and misplaced.

When we had overstayed our welcome there, we decided to get a room at a motel off highway I-70. It was summer, so in Missouri that means hot and extremely humid. Jack had found a job, so I stayed in our tiny motel room with the kids. It wasn't so bad at first. The kids had paper and crayons to color with. They had some of their toys. There was a television.

I dreaded going outside. I tried to stay in as much as possible, at least while Jack was at work. I didn't want anything to do with the outside world. I couldn't believe I was living in a motel room with my children, while crackheads and prostitutes were running amok on the other side of our motel room door. I was relieved to know my children had no concept of the dealings that were going on in that place.

I tried to make it as homey as possible for them.

I kept it clean and made friends with the cleaning ladies. They let me use their supplies so I could clean the room myself. I tried to shield my kids from the corruption and filth all around us. I made the best out of what was given to me. We had a microwave in the room, so that helped with some of the food preparation. We had a mini fridge and a cooler that I was able to keep food and drinks in. I made oatmeal and ramen noodles in the coffee maker. They ate a lot of the cereal my mom had sent with us. I hardly ate anything as usual, my diet was purely liquid.

There were several summer storms that July. That soothed me and made me feel safe and gave me an excuse to hide away. The only day it really bothered me was on the Fourth of July. The last few years the Fourth had been so much fun and held some great memories. Utah has some of the best fireworks displays in the country. We had an incredible view of the entire Salt Lake valley, with fireworks lighting up the sky in every direction. Now, in this dingy motel, on a soggy day, there really was no way to celebrate. We didn't see a single firework, no lit up sky, everything was just dim.

To add to my already crappy mood, a man

drove up to me in his car while I trudged across the parking lot to get some more ice from the ice machine. He began telling me how he had a lady friend who stayed at the motel. He said he'd rather spend his time with me. I was wearing a strapless red dress, an attempt at trying to be somewhat patriotic, and this man had mistaken me for a hooker. Good God. I continued on my way, and he called after me. I turned around and he said his lady friend didn't like the fruity alcoholic beverages he brought. He offered them to me. I'm not one for frilly cocktail drinks bought in bottles, but I accepted them anyway. It was some sort of consolation.

Shortly after Independence Day, we decided that I would go to Kansas City with the kids to stay with my mother-in-law. Jack would stay in Columbia to work. I had reservations, but I couldn't stand to be in that motel anymore. As much as I cleaned, it still felt dirty. My seven-month-old was crawling everywhere and I constantly had to wipe her and change her clothes, because they got dirty so quickly. The atmosphere of that place was starting to drag me down even further than I already was.

We made it to Kansas City, and things weren't too bad. I had some help from my mother-in-law and her friends. I was thankful she had not told me I couldn't drink while staying there. She would allow me some beer. She was afraid that I would experience health complications caused by alcohol withdrawal. I jumped on that idea with enthusiasm, and as I always tended to do, took it too far.

I felt like a burden. I could feel I was not wanted there, not so much with my mother-in-law, but with her husband. His silent looks and behavior were somehow loud. They started fighting more, and at one point I was told that their marriage was being strained by us being there. I felt immense guilt. My children were enjoying their stay, so that made me happy at times. They went to Summer Bible Camp and we planned different activities for them.

A friend of Jack's mom had come by to help me get into a rehab facility. I went with her to different places and a pint of whiskey came with us. I sneaked drinks throughout the day. It seemed that nothing was going right. Everywhere we went, they either couldn't help me, they needed something I didn't have and would take a while to get. We were hitting road blocks everywhere we went. This always happened when I was trying to get help. I knew it was the darkness I always had around me, the devil.

He didn't want me to get better, to grow, to have peace. I was so close to him at this point with all the negativity surrounding me and my thoughts. He didn't want me to get away. His hooves were clenched around my spirit. I still fought it all the time. I fought the feelings of despair and suicide. I couldn't leave my children.

One day the older kids were taken to the movies, and a friend of my mother- in-law's from her church came by. I really liked her. She was a recovering addict and alcoholic, so I felt a connection with her, like she understood. She had brought another lady over, and we were talking. I had already planned to ask them to watch the two little ones, so I could go up the road to get some more cigarettes and go for a walk. The talking was getting to be too much, and I knew I needed something stronger than beer. I wanted vodka.

I left and started on my walk. I walked right past the grocery store, and made my way towards the liquor store. I wandered for a while, knowing I should not buy it, but I had to. Everything was getting to be too much and I just wanted to escape to another world of total and complete oblivion. I bought a gallon of vodka.

As I made my way back, I started to open the seal of the bottle. I was walking behind the grocery store. I needed a drink that minute. It was hotter than hell, I hadn't eaten anything at all, and the dumpster was right beside me, reeking of who knows what. I wanted to vomit right there because of the rancid stench. I told myself no, and I took a swig of the vodka. Now I really wanted to throw up. That wasn't going to happen. I would never waste alcohol that way. I remember thinking to myself, "What the hell are you doing. Look at yourself." I shrugged my shoulders and took another swig, heading back towards the house.

I do not remember too much about what happened next, until the shit hit the fan. My mother-in-law's husband had gone into my room and had thrown all of my things all over the place. He was screaming at me and accusing me of having drugs. I was furious. This little shit just went through all my belongings and was accusing me of something that wasn't true. At least from my perception of what he meant by drugs. I yelled at him to get out and said who knows what. More than likely I said the most hurtful, soul penetrating things that I knew would hurt him. My tongue was always a sharp knife that could cut someone to their core. It was my most useful and effective weapon. I knew I hit some serious buttons when he grabbed my wrists and yelled at me to just shut up. I fought back and he retreated. My mother-in-law had returned with my two oldest kids. She found my vodka and called the police.

I cried and cried, because I had to leave my children at the house and drive away from them in the back of a police car. I cried, because I had crossed the line so drastically, like I always did. I cried, because I couldn't talk myself out of it and make them let me stay. I cried, because I was sad and ashamed, and a horrible mother. I cried, because I was worthless. How and why did I keep doing this to my children? I was angry, because if my shit had just been left alone, none of this would be happening. If he hadn't accused me of having drugs and been so off-putting from the beginning we could have had a peaceful evening. Blaming everyone and everything to make myself feel a little bit better. Placing the blame where it belonged hurt too damn much. I couldn't do it.

The police took me to a rehab and detox center. When I got there, I was silent and brooding.

BRITTANY PRIESTLEY

Everyone was having a discussion about what was going to happen to me next. All I could think about was how I was going to get out of that place. I wanted to go back to my children, but knew I wasn't welcome inside that house.

The counselor talked to me, and I was kind of tuning him out. A nurse started taking my vitals and they had me take a breathalyzer. The police were still there when the counselor came back in to tell me my results. He looked at me strangely, and said, "You should really be in a coma right now. Some people would die with this blood alcohol level. How are you sitting up and talking?" I did not understand a word he was saying. Coma? Die? What? I told him I didn't understand. He told me I blew a 4.8 BAC. The police shook their heads slowly.

I sat there plotting and planning a way to get out of there. I called my parents and told them to get me out. To rescue me from this mess. There was not much they could do. I had to stay until my BAC went down to 1.5. I chugged water and ate saltine crackers. I talked to the counselor. He was nice, an older black man, who had suffered from drug addiction and alcoholism himself. He had been sober for a while at that point. He talked to me about his experiences. He let me go outside and we smoked cigarettes. He told me I could stay there and detox. That they could help.

Without even thinking about it, I told him no. He tried to convince me. At the time I honestly had no idea that my mother-in-law had sent me here to stay and get sober. The thought hadn't even crossed my mind. I was glad to be here as opposed to jail, but that didn't mean I wanted to stay. I was just waiting until they would let me go.

When I finally sobered up enough to be released, I called a taxi cab. I had the driver take me back near my mother-in-law's house. I contemplated trying to go inside to be with my kids. I was so close to them, but worlds away. It broke my heart. I hoped they knew I loved them. I hoped that they knew I didn't do any of this to hurt them. I hope they didn't blame themselves. I prayed to God that they knew these things. I walked alone, in the dark to the grocery store to use the bathroom. I cleaned up a little and put on some make up. I decided I was going to get a few drinks at a bar I had seen down the street. I didn't have much money, but I would figure something out. I sat down at the bar and ordered a beer. I didn't want to think about anything at all. A man was sitting next to me, and we started talking. I knew he would buy me a few drinks. I was all set for a little while longer.

The night went on, and I met some more people. I clicked with some girls and the drinks were coming almost faster than I could drink them. I must have called Jack at some point during that night, because I got several missed calls from him. I was standing outside of the bar at closing time. Those girls I had clicked with earlier were starting to piss me off. For what reason? I don't know. It usually didn't take much. I started talking shit to them, and then Jack pulled into the parking lot. I was shocked by my rescue. He was staying over two hours away and he found me at this random bar. He came just in time, because I was wasted and becoming unruly and mean. He drove to a Walmart parking lot and parked. He had a bottle of vodka in the car, so we drank and hung out for awhile. We hadn't seen each other in a couple of weeks, so there was some catching up to do.

In the morning, I woke up in the car feeling fuzzy and sore. We drove back to Jack's mother's house to pick up the kids. She had a police officer come to make sure everything went alright. To make her feel safe was my assumption. I didn't care, I just wanted to get my kids and get the hell out of there. She wouldn't let me into her house. She had packed up all my things, but I knew she had missed some stuff. She would drive the two-and-a-half hours to bring it back to me at the same motel we had stayed in before. We were still homeless. I couldn't face reality. The motel was now home again, at least for a little while.

CHAPTER FIFTEEN

Unexpected Guardian Angel

I FOUND MYSELF AND MY family back at that damn motel and I asked a question I have asked myself a million times, "How did I end up here?" I couldn't take any of the blame, not this time and hardly ever. This was all Jack's fault. We would never be in this position if he would have just dealt with his issues and stopped running away. It was his mother's fault for a multitude of reasons, spanning back years and years. Everyone's fault, but my own.

I did not want to leave Utah in the first place, and now look where we were. I still tried to make the best out of an extremely undesirable situation.

There was one positive pertaining to the motel. It was summer and they had an outdoor pool. The kids loved the pool and when Jack got off work or had a day off we would all go.

One day Jack had brought us back some huge iced slushy drinks dosed with alcohol from a local place that served only these special drinks. We brought them to the pool with us. We had a good time for a while.

He decided he wanted to go back to the room. He wanted to take the baby with him. He thought it would make it easier for me to watch the other three kids. From what I was told, Jack had stumbled back to the room and almost fell with her in his arms. A woman at the pool witnessed this and called the police. A while later, we were all back at the room and a loud knock came from the door.

When I opened the door, two policemen were standing outside. They asked to talk to my husband. Jack had passed out, so I told them he was sleeping. They said they would talk to me instead. They recounted why they had come by and started questioning me. I told them I was not aware of what happened on his walk back from the pool, but that the baby was alright.

I was drunk and again, I was trying to maintain a calm and respectful demeanor with these cops. They wanted to see the baby, and so I brought her out. They had me sit in the back of the cop car with her, while they looked her over. At that point I was jumping out of my skin. My mantra at that moment was, "Everything is going to be alright, everything is going to be alright." They saw that the baby was fine, and they told me to let my husband sleep it off and to get the kids to bed. I nodded my head yes, and took a deep sigh of relief.

When I got back into the room, I was fuming. I tried to put my feelings aside as I got the kids ready for bed. They were tired from being in the sun and the water, so it didn't take long for them to fall asleep. How dare that woman call the cops? Doesn't she know all the hell we have been going through? Who does she think she is? What a total bitch! I made up my mind that I was going to find her and tell her just exactly what I thought.

There was a party going on by the pool with people drinking and listening to loud music. The Show-Me State Games were being held in Columbia that weekend, so people traveled from all over to attend. By this time, I was super drunk. Drunk on fury, anger, vengeance, liquor. I sought to find that woman and I found her almost immediately. I walked over to her and all I said was, "I hope you know that karma is a bitch, and you will get everything that's coming to you." She looked at me shocked and I turned to walk away. It is possible I could have said more, but I don't remember that part.

The next minute there were four African American women, one being the woman I had just talked to, coming right at me. The next thing I remember was one of them hitting me, and I hit her back. They all jumped in to start an unfair fight, but I suppose I had started it.

Next, I was on the ground trying to shield the punches and kicks that landed everywhere. I kept thinking they were going to beat me to death. I laid there for I don't know how long, having the crap beat out of me. I had not been beat up by a girl before, and definitely not by several at once.

There came a moment of complete silence, which I found odd, so I opened my eyes. I looked up and saw a man, and he had light shining behind him. It was probably light from a street lamp, but nonetheless he shined brightly in a very dim situation. He was a tall, slim African American man wearing a white t-shirt. He reached down to me with both hands, as if he moved in slow motion. Everything was so still and quiet amid a time of complete violence and chaos. An instantaneous peace ran throughout my whole body, which at that point had been severely beaten and bruised. He held my hands in his own and lifted me up, and all he said was, "Run!"

I remember running back to my motel room where my kids were sleeping. I kept looking back over and over again as I ran, wanting to get away as quickly as possible, but also wanting another glimpse of the man who just helped me. I couldn't see much, my vision too blurry from tears. I was bawling as I ran, but all I could think about was that man. He saved my life. The word Guardian Angel popped into my head. I got to the room, full of everyone I loved dearly and was so happy to be back in that dingy room I had grown to despise. I passed out immediately.

I woke up the next morning to Jack, angry and violent. He couldn't quite remember the events from the day or night before, but he knew something had gone wrong. In his mind I was always the culprit. I was always the one to blame, I always caused trouble, I could never just keep my mouth shut, I always drank too much and had to cause a scene. Sometimes that was the truth. There was even a little bit of truth to that just the day before. When he was sleeping, passed out and drunk, he had no idea what I dealt with. I had basically saved his ass with the cops the night before. It was me who had to deal with his actions, always trying to pick up the pieces of the shit storm that had blown through. Dealing with the aftermath and doing damage control, as I often referred to it.

I always thought it must be so easy to just black out and not remember anything. I strove for that with every sip, every inhale, every snort, every swallow I ever took. I just wanted to forget and float in an alternate reality of complete and blissful ignorance. Rarely, if ever did that happen. I would forget snippets here and there, but as the day went on, flashbacks from the night before kept coming back, creeping their way back into my mind. Each flashback made my need to escape ever more pressing. Not ever wanting to deal with anything, and never even knowing how to or where to start.

When he woke up the first thing he did was yell

at me and punch me in my eye. It always had to be that damn eye. The sound of ringing and static noise that I had heard many times appeared. I couldn't believe it. What had I done? I started crying, cringing as I looked at myself in the mirror. Flashbacks from every other hit or hurtful word started coming back, as usual. I did everything wrong. I just couldn't seem to get it right. I tried to be a good wife, a good mother. I no longer sought perfection, because I knew I was too far gone to even try. I couldn't even fake it anymore. It had all become too exhausting.

I tried so hard to protect my children from the harsh, scary world where people used, abused, and took what they wanted from you when they wanted it. I thought that if they knew and could feel how much I truly cherished and loved them, that would make all the times they had seen me intoxicated and unruly to other people not seem so bad. I was not abusive to my children, but they were witness to my abuse of others, and definitely the abuse that was inflicted on me. I was not a good role model. I was teaching them all the wrong lessons. I was showing them how to be like me, and I didn't want that for them. I wanted them to be the better version of myself. The me I never had a chance to become.

I tried to protect them from the outside, strangers and the like, but really all along I had been inviting the danger into my own home. The scary monsters were living with us. I had become one of them. We could no longer stay at the motel. I had gotten us kicked out of a place where drug dealers, drug addicts, and prostitutes were more than welcome. Why had that man saved me? I didn't deserve to be rescued. I had become the lowest of the low.

CHAPTER SIXTEEN

Kaleidoscope Eyes

EVERY DAY BEFORE JACK LEFT for work, I would make sure he had left me enough beer to last until he returned home. I usually had more hidden in various places throughout the house, the only problem was there were times I couldn't remember where I had hidden them. I tried to stick to beer during the day, so I didn't get wasted. I tried to stick with beer, period. Hard alcohol always took me to a level where I had no business being. Nonetheless, I tried.

It was a spring day, in late March. We had been

living in this new house for six months, three of which I had been sober from alcohol. I took Antabuse, thinking that was my solution. It was not. On this spring day, I was horrified to find that I had been left with nothing to help get me through the day. I had the shakes and I was out of my mind about not having something, anything to get me away from myself. I felt abandoned and left to deal with life alone. My normal state of anxiety was now propelled to a state of panic. I fought hard to maintain an outward appearance of assurance that I could handle the day, but inside I was dismantling.

It was a beautiful day, with clear and sunny skies. I took the kids out back to play in the yard. I sat on the steps connected to the back deck, lit a cigarette, put on some music, and watched as they played. I had settled down a bit, but then something strange started happening.

As I was looking out into the yard, I started seeing a rainbow of colors circling and circling around where my irises and pupils are, but projected out into thin air. They would trail and go in whichever direction I happened to glance. I started closing and opening my eyes repeatedly to see if the spinning circles of color would go away, but they remained, spinning beautifully.

I was instantly reminded of the hallucinations I would experience when I took shrooms. I had taken magic mushrooms more times than I can remember. At times, even now, if I stared at something long enough, like a tree trunk or a wooden table or floor, I could see the motions and patterns I would see while tripping. I thought about that, and thought to myself that this was kind of amazing. That turned to confusion quickly. I couldn't be tripping or hallucinating, because I hadn't taken anything, not even one drink.

The next thing I knew I was being woken up by Jack. I was disoriented and my bottom lip was hurting and swollen. I had no idea what was going on. The last thing I remember was being outside with kaleidoscope eyes. He kept asking me questions about what happened and if I was alright. I had no memory of what had happened. I still do not know what took place that day or how I got back inside the house. I couldn't remember what day it was, but I vaguely remembered who the president of the United States was. I wondered why he was asking me all these random questions.

I needed to get away to be alone for a minute. I

said I needed to use the bathroom. I walked to the back of the house, went into the bathroom, and shut and locked the door behind me. I walked to the sink and looked at myself in the mirror. I felt like I was watching from outside myself, looking at myself looking into my bathroom mirror. I was disheveled and my lip was bruised and swollen. I had bitten my own lip.

I remember looking at myself in bewilderment and coming to the stark realization that something was very very wrong. I turned to walk out and I took a deep breath. I was attempting to do what I do best and push down any feelings of unease and discomfort.

That didn't work, so I walked back to the kitchen and grabbed a beer. Jack had bought some on his way home. I had called him several times that day demanding that he come home early with beer, so he did. Jack didn't think it was a good idea to drink, but he had learned a long time ago to not get in between alcohol and me. He said I needed to go see our physician. I promised I would, not really meaning it, as I took a sip of beer. He grabbed the phone and dialed the doctor's office.

I had my appointment the next day. My

physician knew that I was an alcoholic. I had been to see him several times. He was also a friend of Bill W. and I had gone to meetings with his recommendation and seen him there. He had also prescribed me Antabuse, a medication to deter one from drinking alcohol by making one violently sick if they should drink. I tested that theory once.

I had slowly stopped taking them and after about five days without it, I decided to drink. I broke out in hives everywhere. Jack came home and stated, "You drank, didn't you." He didn't even need to ask, but I lied anyway. He knew the truth. He told me what I had experienced in the backyard the day before sounded an awful lot like a seizure caused by alcohol withdrawal. He ordered lab tests on my liver and said he would call me with the results.

A couple of days passed, and it was a beautiful weekend. The weather was still nice and we took the kids out to go on a hike to a place called The Devil's Icebox. We had a good time, being outside in the fresh air. We walked and the kids got to go into a cave that had a small lake of water surrounding it. They played and enjoyed the water while I took pictures. From the outside it all looked perfect, just the way I always tried to make it seem. I had really put in an effort to not drink. I had accepted that I was an alcoholic a long time before this, I had accepted that my life was a mess at times due to my drinking, but I finally came to the conclusion that perhaps alcohol was taking a toll on me, physically.

For whatever reason, I thought my body could withstand the damage I inflicted on it. The abuse. I had dealt with abuse my entire life; molestation, emotional, physical, spiritual, mental, psychological abuse, rape. I was the worst abuser of them all. The years of not taking care of my body, the drug addiction – weed, cocaine, ecstasy, shrooms, cigarettes, my pill popping, and the booze that washed it all down. Alcohol was with me every step of the way. Alcohol had been my best friend, always there for me whenever I wanted or needed it, for a little over half of my life.

On the drive home from the hike my phone rang. I didn't need to look at the phone. I knew who was calling. I answered it hesitantly. "Hello?" It was my doctor and he began to speak. With every word he was saying, my eyes started to fill with tears a little more. I remained intact for the duration of the phone call and when I hung up, I burst into hysterical tears. I was never one who liked to cry and every time I knew I was about to, I'd fight it with all my might. When Jack looked over at me he knew it was not good news. I told him through sobs as best I could, that I had damage to the liver; my enzymes were 400 percent higher than they should be. I needed to stop drinking. If I did not quit drinking alcohol I would be lucky if I made it to the age of forty. I was thirty-one at the time.

I had my whole family in the car—my husband, my four beautiful children, the oldest six and the youngest one, with a five and three year old in between. I started calculating what ages they would be. How old would my children be when they lost their mother? I cried harder. I never wanted to be without my children. I immediately pushed thoughts of my death out of my mind the instant they tried to creep in. Unimaginable.

I loved them; infinite and indescribable is the love a mother has for her children. I had already learned that sometimes love wasn't enough. Wasn't enough to save me from myself from slowly starving myself and drinking myself to death.

Hadn't I wished for death a million times? I think that's one reason why the saying "Be careful what you wish for" is always so foreboding. Sometimes what you wished for, you do not want anymore. I did not want to be the woman I heard so many stories about. The tragic story of the woman who didn't stop and died so young. What a waste.

I didn't want to be a waste. I didn't want my children to be looked at with pity, or believe that they weren't good enough for me to want to stick around and live for them. I wanted to be with them and create memories they would hold dear forever, so that when I did die peacefully in old age, they would smile and laugh, not cry and be filled with sorrow.

I decided I was really going to try. I remember praying to God and asking Him for strength, actually I told Him I was strong and that I could do this on my own. I always believed in God, but my biggest flaw was thinking I knew better than God. I thought if I was just self-sufficient enough and determined enough that I, and I alone, could conquer this massive obstacle. I prayed for Him to help me do what I needed to do to get better. That was my first mistake. I couldn't do anything for myself.

I had already proven to be my own worst enemy, who made the worst possible choices concerning my own well-being. I set out on this path of righting years of distorted beliefs. I sent Jack to pick up my prescription of Antabuse. I had gone five days without a drink. He came home and literally placed the Antabuse and a bottle of vodka on the countertop. I had a choice, and the choice I made was mine and mine alone. If history is any indicator of future events, and of the choice I was to make, I bet you can guess which one I chose.

MOMMY DRUNKEST

* * *

Coming Around Again, February?

Heartache is an unexplainable tragedy. It pokes at the mind until the only rhythm you can feel is his body's movements. It's all an illusion, a dirty trick your mind plays on you. A repeated beating, the abusive beating of the heart that leaves deep scars. Such a tease to see his face, remember his touch, the tone of his voice. The smiles and look in his eyes. It's a burden I put on myself, because I remember.

Memories are good and I keep many stored in this head of mine. Sometimes the greatest memories become the most wicked. It's the great ones that keep you holding on, believing someday you can once again obtain them. Isn't it nonsense to put faith in a scene that reels through the mind? No sure foundation or concrete evidence that it will ever be yours.

Yet, I hold on to the desperate wanting of having my past as my future. I hold on to every word, every minute, every breath. I keep holding onto him. It's hard to hold tight to something I never did have a grasp on. The memories are thought of and never reconciled. I'm constantly thirsty and never replenished.

If I had the chance to erase him from my mind, along with all the disgustingly precious memories I keep, I would not. Although I'm hurt and sore, although I have no appetite. I would never want to forget. The good outweighs the bad, if that's even believable. In the end, I have to have him. If not, I feel I won't ever be truly happy.

To think I had him in the palm of my hand and I let him go. Without realizing what had happened, only deepens my anguish and hardens my depression rendering it stone. Lifeless, just a blank expression staring through nothingness floating into eternity. My blank expression as I remember everything.

If he knew how badly I wanted him to be only mine, I feared he would run to a safer girl. He ran away anyway, without a backward glance or a second thought. He dusted me off. The dead skin blew away to unveil a new him and a new me, without each other. All I had left were memories and dreams, and even in some of my own dreams I couldn't have him. Always out of reach.

BRITTANY PRIESTLEY

"It sometimes happens that a man and a woman meet and instantly recognize the other half of themselves behind the eyes of each other. The eyes have been said to be 'the windows of the soul.' Even their voices sound familiar to each other's ears, like a remembered chord of music. These are two who immediately sense the unalterable fact that they have been—are—and must be One; even though they might have fought against their fate for centuries and struggled in vain to escape their linked destiny. Almost from the first moment they meet and gaze upon each other, their spirits rush together in joyful recognition, ignoring all convention and custom, all social rules of behavior, driven by an inner knowing too overwhelming to be denied. Inexplicably, often without a word spoken, they know that only through each other can they hope to be complete in every way"
    -Linda Goodman

MOMMY DRUNKEST

I think I have found him, but for now he is out of reach. I hurt him and he hurts me. Misunderstanding and misconduct are the culprits. There is the fear of being hurt and that fear only brings more pain and holds us back. I brought it all upon myself.

What they say is true, about time healing all wounds. Although I could never be fully over him, I was no longer consumed. I saw others, but no one compared. I grabbed on to anything that would take my mind away. An allowance to escape my heartbreak. Then I saw him again. In that moment, I couldn't resist. We finally woke up and did so together. Absolutely remarkable. Deep and fulfilling. We had reunited. At night he poured his water for us to share. Candlelight and the moon shining through a window above our heads.

He looked into my eyes and I saw something. It only lasted a split second, but time had frozen and that something was forever. Misunderstanding won again, and I was the one who suffered. There was no special connection. I could have been wrong. Once again he was gone, but only to return again.

***

BRITTANY PRIESTLEY

MOMMY DRUNKEST

February came back again.

To put me out, to wear me thin.

I'm tired of its constant rain.

Wet seeps through my pores, makes me feel the pain.

It's cold and bitter.

Nothing to do but sit here.

I wait and wait for the sun's light.

February doesn't bring it to my life.

He is a month that always returns,

Only with actions and hidden words.

His clouds cover my sun

And when I think it's over, it's never truly done.

The month will go and his impressions remain there.

As a new month comes, I hope I don't care.

I know February will once again return.

This time it won't put me out, This time I'll make it burn.

CHAPTER SEVENTEEN

Demons are Here; The End is Near

WHEN I MADE THE DECISION to choose vodka over Antabuse, life got hellish rather quickly. Many of the living nightmares that were to come in the next few weeks I had experienced before. Anytime I anticipated the alcohol and pills, (anything that made me feel comfort), were about to be ripped from my life I would clasp on with a tighter grip.

It was as if the world were ending and I had one last chance to guzzle and put into my body whatever

I could before time ran out. I didn't stop drinking, not even for an hour. Budweiser was my water and vodka was there to pick my buzz up more quickly. I clung to them like a baby to a bottle, like my life depended on it. I think it did.

I would wake up in the morning and chug a beer or two before taking my daughter to the bus stop for school. I woke in the middle of the night to have a beer or take a shot, usually after having terrifying nightmares that I could no longer forget and drown with liquor and pills. They came on more vividly and real than ever. I could no longer escape my reality, and my reality had turned into hell. The only solution I had was to drink more, take more of whatever I had stashed around the house. There had to be some way to make it all stop.

* * *

I am taking a moment outside of what happened at this time in my life, to take note and let you know what happened while I was writing this story. I am sitting in the same living room writing this now that I was in when this story took place. This is where I witnessed a congregation of dark shadows, demons, evil entities, whatever you prefer to call them. As I was writing this, I noticed the number of words not changing with every word I wrote. I went to leave the document so it would refresh, knowing I always keep auto save on. This was my sixteenth story. When I came back to continue writing, everything I had written past the first paragraph had completely vanished. I looked everywhere in my documents and found nothing. I wrote to Adam and confided in him about what had just happened. He told me demons hate it when we tell our story. They hate a story that will glorify God. Demons wanted me to stop and give up. A red blip showed up in my title on the word demons. I deleted the whole title and typed it again. I went to delete the word demon, but the red mark wouldn't go away. I continued writing and when I scrolled back up, the red blip had finally vanished. Evil didn't want me to show anyone the grace and mercy I have received from God. A message of hope for people who feel like they have none. A message that people don't have to dig themselves to the hellish depths of despair that some of us do. First God, and then one's own self can aid in the climb out of darkness to enjoy a life of love, peace, and fulfilling purpose. Spiritual warfare is real and happening all around us. Some are attuned to it a little more, but I think we can all sense it happening at certain points in our lives. I have felt opposition in my life. I felt it a lot in the process of writing this book. I have been seeking a stronger connection to God, Jesus Christ, and the Holy Spirit at this juncture. Trying to turn all of myself over to Him for my protection and care and letting go of that tiny bit of self I've been holding on to. I believe it's at this point the devil attempts to regain his utter control with swift desperation. God and I won't let it happen. I won't give up. I was never one to hesitate before the dark wall of the devil. I didn't give up no matter how dark my life got or how close I drove to the gates of hell. That's my story, and I'll continue to tell it.

* * *

I BECAME A TOTAL RECLUSE, hiding away from the world and keeping the world safe from me. I didn't trust myself anymore. I lived in a constant state of fear. Fear of life, fear of death, fear for my children and their happiness and safety. Fear of my husband.

The only times I did leave the house were to go to the bus stop to pick up my daughter after school. One other time I left my kids alone at home to go buy some alcohol. I had already been drinking, and so I thought it better to go and leave them for a few minutes as opposed to having them drive with me behind the wheel, drunk. I bribed them with promises of candy and treats. I knew it was wrong, but I did it anyway. Nothing could come between me and what I needed to survive another minute of another day. Even if and when it was killing me.

I had to steer clear of most of our neighbors. I had bad blood with almost every one of them. My anger and misery perpetuated every relationship or simple conversation I had with other people. I couldn't quite keep my thoughts to myself, and like I said, I always knew how to cut someone to the core using my blunt mouth like a knife. Always bringing their deepest darkest secrets and fears to the surface to turn around and smack them in the face.

One neighbor, who had become somewhat of a friend wanted nothing to do with me anymore. She had supplied me with all kinds of pills throughout our friendship. She had known me while I had been sober from alcohol for about three months while I was taking Antabuse, but she saw a drastic change in me that wasn't likable in any way whatsoever.

She always gave me a strange vibe. I didn't ever feel completely comfortable with her, even though I should have. She understood the things unseen that I could see and feel. She read me tarot cards. Her house gave me the creeps and I told her so. Every time I went in there I could sense the man that had died in that house and his spirit still remained. She validated what I told her and told me about the man who had a heart attack and died there. When she realized I had certain gifts and she knew I was an empath, she asked me to be her fourth. Some sort of Wiccan term that gave me an unnerved feeling, so I declined.

One night I attempted to get out of my house and run to hers. Jack and I had been drinking and fighting. I just wanted to leave and get away from him, but he didn't want to let me go. He grabbed the back of my head by my hair and smashed my head into the wall. My forehead was gouged by a sharp bracket that had been stuck in the wall. I got away and ran to her house with blood dripping down my face, crying hysterically. I became too much, was always too much for people. Nobody wants to deal with a mess of a person, and that's exactly what I was. A complete mess.

I honestly don't know how I managed anything during this time. I don't know how I took care of my kids. I took care of them the best that I was able to, but I know that wasn't enough. I did the bare minimum; it was all I could muster. This hurts me to admit, still to this day, but I was neglectful of my children. I was so stuck in a state of emptiness, devoid of any light.

I felt encompassed and shrouded by darkness. I let my kids do as they pleased, just so I didn't have to deal with them. As long as I wasn't annoyed or bothered I didn't care. I'd get angry if they did something that crossed the line, like fighting or breaking their toys. In actuality I had become angry with myself for not having the energy to guide them and help them. I did sometimes, but more often I did not. I truly believe that God was with and around my children all the time. I thank God every day, still to this day that nothing tragic ever happened to my children. So many times, so many things could have gone miserably wrong. They were kept safe. God was doing for my children what I could not.

I prayed so much during this time. I hated that I

found myself praying more when life was horrible and I needed something from God. I wished I could've been more grateful than I was, but I took everything, everyone, and every blessing for granted. I remember saying two specific prayers many times a day. The first was to be with and protect my kids from any harm. I prayed for their safety, happiness, and health. The second I said more often: I prayed to survive each day. Something kept scratching at my subconscious. I intuitively knew an end was coming. I didn't know what the end was going to look like or be, but a storm was brewing and just like before the rain comes, I sensed it.

    I experienced a complete depletion of energy. Sometimes I was afraid to lie down, because when I did I literally could not get back up. This was not the inability to get out of bed caused by depression. I had experienced that as well. This was something different. It felt like something I could not see was sitting on my chest. The best way I can describe it is by saying it felt like a solid mass that had me pinned. I tried to move and wiggle myself free, but exhaustion came too quickly. Physically I felt null and void. I never knew how long I would stay like that, but I tried to avoid lying down as much as I possibly could. Physically, I could not find the strength or motivation to even get in the shower.

I spent most of the day saying the second prayer. I would say, "Dear Heavenly Father, please just get me through this day. Please just let me survive today. I say these words in the name of Jesus Christ. Amen." I prayed over and over for God to help me live another day, just to get me through one more day. My innermost self knew I couldn't go on like this much longer. My innermost self did not want to die.

That All Knowing Light that I believe is inherent to every human being and resides in our souls was muffled, diluted, drugged, poisoned, and I could hardly hear it, but for once I was trying to listen. I knew I had come to a point of no return. I would sit with my children as they slept and weep. I was filled to the brim with so much regret, shame, remorse, and I just felt hollowed. Like everything that was or ever could be good in me was gone. No trace of the real and true me to be found.

At this point I had been throwing up more than usual. I couldn't control it. My body was physically rejecting the substances I was forcing into it. After I would throw up, I would grab the vodka, plug my nose so my sense of smell and taste was deadened, take a swig, and have a gum or mint ready to put in my mouth immediately after, keeping my nose plugged for at least a minute so I couldn't taste the vodka, making it bearable so I could keep it down. Sick insanity is what that's called. I never ate and bile would sink to the bottom of the toilet or drain down the sink. For a while now, at this point, it wasn't just liquor and stomach acid I was throwing up. I was throwing up blood.

In April of 2017, I had one of the most spiritually terrifying experiences of my life. One day I found myself at home alone. This rarely, if ever, happened. There was usually at least one child at home with me, typically the baby. I remember waking up to my empty house, having no clue where anyone was. I didn't know where they'd gone. I couldn't remember the last time I saw them. I completely panicked. I had an overwhelming feeling of dread.

I felt like the world was closing in on me and I was going to experience complete darkness at any moment. I kept thinking, "This is it. I'm going to die. Alone, in my house in the middle of the day, and my whole family is going to come home and find me here." I was in my kitchen calling people frantically. I just wanted to reach someone, anyone. No one answered. I left a few voice messages explaining how scared I was and that I really needed help. I had never felt the gravity of the world pulling on me like that but in retrospect, I don't believe it was a force from this world that had me out of my mind.

I couldn't see my living room from my kitchen, but I could feel it. It sent chills throughout my entire body, engulfing me with every morbid, disturbing, dark, evil feeling all at once .Whatever this energy was, it was strong. I felt pulled to it. It was calling me to come, and the temptation to go was too much for me to resist. Every part of me did not want to see what was in that room, but once again there I was, feeling completely helpless and once again letting things happen to me. A passenger, not the driving force of my own life.

I had seen a lot of strange things throughout my life, but what I saw when I crept around the corner into the living room was nothing I had ever seen before and I haven't seen anything like it since. Thank you, God. My living room was filled with dark shadows that resembled men, but had no distinct features. No faces, just the shapes of men.

They were blurry and indistinct, but I knew what they were. I kept blinking quickly thinking they would vanish every time I reopened my eyes, but they remained standing in a sort of congregation. I knew why they were here in my home. They wanted me and I felt like death had come to collect me, or to warn me that it was coming soon. I stood frozen and paralyzed. This was the end I had been dreading. That ominous feeling that had accompanied me every day and every night for the last few weeks. This was the storm I could sense coming.

I wouldn't tell a living soul about the demons I saw for another year. I don't remember them leaving or me walking away from them. I honestly don't remember the rest of that day. I just knew I had danced with the devil a few too many times. Now he was sending for me. I prayed and I prayed and I prayed, and I hoped that it would help.

The end I had been dreading arrived two days later. It wouldn't be the death of my body, but it would be the end of something I loved more than my own life. It is what we in the addiction community refer to as our rock bottom, and mine took with it my heart. Turns out there can be a fate worse than death. At the time I would see it as a curse and a punishment. I believe God always knows what I need. I would later come to believe it was my greatest blessing. It was exactly what I needed, in order to save my own life.

MOMMY DRUNKEST

Hung

Lost in this lonely race
The road is winding, slows down my pace
I wonder if I'll ever come in first place
Exhausted by the non-stop run
My heart is melting, I've been hung
I wonder when will it ever be done
Will you cut this string?
Or leave me here hanging free?
There is no such thing as a man
Only small boys with burly hands

CHAPTER EIGHTEEN

Twenty Months Without a Heart

THE POLICE OF OUR SMALL town in Missouri knew me and Jack from an extensive past of bad decisions, made on behalf of our alcoholism. The day my rock bottom arrived was just about the same. The same as all the other times Jack and I both drank, and one didn't slow down to be somewhat in touch with reality.

On this particular day, Jack had gotten upset about something, I don't even remember what. He had been yelling and he broke a window that was attached to our basement. He would later try to blame me for that window breaking, but I had learned my lesson when it came to punching out windows. The neighbors had seen this and called the police.

When the police showed up, I was drunk, but not unruly yet. I had bruises on my face and I still had the gash on my forehead. They already knew about our domestic violence issues, but I lied about it. I tried to blame a neighbor for my injuries. My children were inside with some other police officers and Jack. I was being questioned outside.

When the moment came that I realized I was going to be arrested, I lost it. I screamed for my children and wanted to at least hug them goodbye. I had tears running down my face and I was struggling to get to them. A few cops had to restrain me. I was put in handcuffs and placed in the back of a police car. I got the handcuffs under my legs and in front of me, and I tried to get through the tiny window to the front of the cop car. I got through it and tried to climb onto the driver seat and out of the driver seat door, but the cop was well equipped and trained in dealings with lunatics.

That was how I was acting, insane with fright

and unable to comprehend what was happening and all the consequences that were to follow. I honestly thought I could convince the cops to let me stay home with my kids. I hadn't learned how to deal with real consequences. This time I would have to pay. For reasons still unknown to me, Jack told the police there was no one that could take the kids while we were both in jail. The state became responsible for them.

The fear and confusion they must have experienced during this time makes me sick down to my soul. I can't dwell on these thoughts for any amount of time, really. I felt such tremendous guilt for having put them, still innocent in so many ways, through such horrible circumstances. I have forgiven myself and I believe they have too. If in the future I should find they have not, I will spend the rest of my life making it right. The first way I can do that is to remain sober.

I got combative with the police officers as they were taking me into the station, where they were about to confine me to a cage. One female cop really let me have it. I don't remember being in the jail cell, but I do remember being bailed out and leaving. Jack had gotten us both bailed out. I don't even think I tried to call anyone. I had probably lost that right with my outrageous behavior.

The moment I returned home I began bawling. I felt my kids' presence missing in every quiet corner in every quiet room. All of my happy memories resurfacing at the most inopportune time. I cried that my children were gone. I didn't know what to do, so I took a shot. It was 2:00 a.m. and I drank until I passed out.

The next morning when I came to, reality hit me like a ton of bricks. We spent the day trying to figure out where the kids had been placed. A family member I will call Sue, helped us to track them down. I spent that day attempting to drink my new wounds into evasive numbness. The pain hadn't yet set in. My mind wouldn't allow it.

Sue arrived at our house and she planned on taking me and Jack to the hospital. I honestly thought I was going there to get rehydrated, and then they would send me on my merry way. I had already been drinking all morning. Right before we left I chugged a can of Budweiser, and that would be my last drink.

The first hospital didn't want to admit me, so I took that as a sign I wasn't supposed to be doing this. I now know that is exactly why I had to keep trying. I wanted to give up and go home. I needed a drink. I talked to my dad on the phone in the parking lot of the second hospital. He was crying and begging me to stay there and get help. He didn't want me to die. I still didn't understand what all the fuss was about. I finally relented after hours of persuasion and pleas from several loved ones.

My purpose for being there became abundantly clear. I detoxed at the hospital for two days. The detox was rough. The hardest part was reliving the memories of bringing my four children into this world in hospital rooms just like this one. I didn't know what my world would be like if I couldn't have them in it.

April 14, 2017 was the first day I went without a drink or any other substance. As soon as I was discharged I was taken directly to an addiction recovery center called Valley Hope. This was my second visit to this facility, but that first attempt had only lasted a couple of hours. I spent four more days in detox there, and total of thirty days at the facility. I cried most of the time. All my pent up tears streamed endlessly. I also laughed harder than I had in years, making my stomach hurt. I was actually feeling true emotions that weren't manifesting themselves as anger.

I attended meetings at a 12-step program, which many who attend called the Fellowship. I received my 30 Day coin on Mother's Day. I saw that as a sign from God that I was starting on the true path that had always been intended for me. It gave me hope and strength that I could stay sober for my children. That's all I needed at that time to keep going. I did everything that was suggested of me. I wasn't afraid to ask for help, because I had learned along the way it wasn't a sign of weakness. The only way I would get help was by asking for it.

I started working with a sort of mentor in the program and we started to go through the steps together. I am forever grateful for that amazing woman. I started early in my sobriety doing service work for the group and other people in the fellowship. I finally came to the realization that I wasn't owed a damn thing. The more I gave, the more I would receive. I always knew I was meant to help people. It has given me a great sense of joy and fulfillment in my life today.

I owe the Fellowship for my life, for a strong foundation that I have built my recovery upon, for support, for teaching me that I am my own problem as well as my own solution, true and authentic relationships with others, and lessons in humility (which I greatly needed).

Most importantly, the program allowed me to change my relationship with God. I always believed in God, but my hang-up was thinking I knew better than Him. I thought I could play God. I spent over half of my life trying to live in a reality that didn't exist. A reality where I was in control of everything and everyone. God waited patiently for me to realize I only needed to rely on Him. He has always been with me, especially in my darkest times.

MOMMY DRUNKEST

***

A Sobering Message

I take no pride in saying I have been arrested, and I cannot tell you the number of times I have been put under lock and key. Each one of these occurrences seems to blur into the next and swirls its way back around to the beginning. The only time I remember believing I would do anything in my power to ensure this would not happen again, was the only time I sat in jail stone cold sober.

I will just say a lot of rippling effects had taken place for me to be put under arrest while in rehab. I had been a resident for eight days. It was a Saturday, the sun high in the sky without a cloud to be seen. I was enjoying conversation with my fellows when the reality of the outside world crept in with a uniform and a badge. Devastation and shock coursed through me. The same police officer, who had arrested me weeks earlier and who completely obliterated my entire life, strolled towards me. Just lovely.

I carried a deep resentment for law

enforcement. They always knew how to ruin my day by taking me away and placing me inside a cage. They were the problem, not me. Today, I know what a lie that is. Today, I would look each one in the eyes, shake their hand, apologize profusely, and thank them for protecting other people from me and me from myself. I hadn't yet come to that understanding at the time. I was still the prodigal victim.

I was crying, but I remained calm. He put the handcuffs on me and put me in the back of the police car, while patients and staff looked on. I cried in the backseat. I put up no fight. I sobbed, "I don't belong in jail. I belong in treatment. That is where I need to be." The officer replied, "I know that, and I'm sorry. It's the judge's order." I had a warrant out for my arrest—violation of unsupervised probation. Turns out it's all the same in the end. The police officer was kind. He allowed me to smoke a cigarette before taking me in. He kept looking at me as I smoked. He finally said, "You know, you're an entirely different person from the last time I saw you." I looked back at him and said, "I know."

When we walked through the doors I saw Jack sitting on a bench, hands bound behind him in handcuffs. They had arrested him as well. The sadness and disappointment that passed between us was palpable. What had we done? We really knew how to destroy everything. I was instructed to not look at him. We had a no contact order placed on us. It was all so surreal. Being sober made me feel out of sorts in this environment. This was not the way it usually went.

I was put in a cell with another woman, who seemed nice enough. We talked and she spoke about God a lot. The whole situation was terrible, but I figured someone would bail me out. I was actually able to lie down and sleep. That rest was shattered rather quickly.

I heard the screaming before I saw the woman behind it. The steel door opened and in stumbled a woman I will never forget. This woman would have been pretty if she weren't so ugly. She was shrouded in darkness and sucked the life out of the tiny room. She was ranting and raving. Completely out of her mind. Stark raving mad.

She started screaming to Jesus. I will not even repeat what she rambled on and on about. What she was saying was so profane, derogatory, wicked. It was hard to listen to. As she was screaming all these horrific things about Jesus, she began washing her feet and hands in the toilet bowl. She was washing herself, and it was almost like a baptismal scene. She took the toilet water in her hands and washed it over her head and all through her hair. She stripped naked and continued in this mad charade and I couldn't divert my eyes.

The whole time I was repeating, "Thank God that isn't me. Thank you God, that that is not me." Then it hit me like a soft blow. I knew that if I had kept traveling that road to hell, like I'd always done, that would have been me. I was watching this, and I could finally see. I could see the fork in the road. I felt for the first time, in a very long time, that I had a choice.

Life wasn't something that just happened to me, rendering me helpless. I heard, "Do you want that for yourself?" I screamed silently, "No, God. Please, no." I believe God showed me all of this right when I could see it. I would do anything to have God's light surrounding me. I could not stand the numbing shadows blanketing me any longer. I got bailed out and I went straight back to rehab.

***

MY RELIANCE ON GOD WOULD become my saving grace for the next twenty months. My husband and I had given temporary guardianship of our children to a family member, the one I call Sue. We wanted to do what was best for the kids. This way they would be with family, and they would not be separated from one another. In all honesty, my initial feeling was total resistance, but I really had no choice.

I signed the papers while I was still in rehab. The deal was she would have help from another family member in a different state while Jack and I worked on our sobriety and recovery. We would have monthly visits, but they would live with her for a year. That seemed so long, but I had a lot of healing and work to do to get better. I knew I had been sick for a very long time. We would have FaceTime calls and I would have access to my own children. That plan worked out for only a couple of months.

The things I had worried about with this agreement finally started to happen. Power trips, control, taking advantage of this situation when I was in the most weak and fragile state of my life. Sue told me I would never make it. She said I would relapse and drink again. I decided then and there I would stay sober. Not to prove her wrong, but for my children and for my life.

In sobriety, I have learned there are people who believe you will succeed. There are the people who want you to succeed. Ones who don't believe you will succeed. Then there are those who do not want you to succeed. I find it extremely important to figure out who is who. I found Sue to be in the last category. I don't want to get into the negativity too much here. I have wasted enough time on negativity and my feelings surrounding this situation.

Because of all this discord, Jack and I were only able to see our children on two different occasions during this time. We had last seen them in September of 2017. I would not see them all together again, face to face, until December of 2018.

I would not be allowed to call and talk to them when I wanted to, even just to say "I love you and night night." That was dictated and controlled by their temporary guardian. It was a set schedule, which sometimes got cancelled when we said something we weren't supposed to, like, "We really miss you and love you guys." That made it harder for the adults who cared for the children when we said things like this. They might actually have had to deal with their emotions, and refrain from treating them like militaristic robots.

I saw my youngest child when she had her adenoids removed in December of 2017. Jack and I drove two hours to Kansas City to be with her before the procedure and for about forty-five minutes after it had been done. We had to say goodbye there at the surgical center. I was not able to take care of her. She was two. I bawled my eyes out as we drove back home.

I missed every holiday with my kids during this time. I missed their birthdays. I celebrated my youngest child's first birthday with her and wouldn't again until she turned four. It was absolutely heartbreaking.

I did not physically see or speak to my younger son for an entire year. Not even on FaceTime. He cried too much after he talked to us. Sue claimed it was because of the trauma he endured. I knew it was because he was a little three-year-old boy who wanted and missed his mother. It is hard for people to recognize things such as these when they themselves have never loved.

The guardian wouldn't allow them to see us. There was always a different excuse. I knew she was up to no good. We had no access to their medical records or the help they were receiving from therapists. Sue had complete power to control and contort whatever stories she wanted to tell about myself, my children, and their father. No one seemed to think it was of any importance to see what the parents had to say.

The guardian seemed to have conveniently forgotten that we still had all of our parental rights. I cringe when I think of all the lies she told about me. I've learned that what other people say about me is none of my business. It really says more about the slanderer than it actually says about me.

I know somewhere in her mind she thought she was helping, but her help just hurt. It hurt everyone involved, especially my children. I have always known the truth and I knew the truth would come out eventually. I just had to be patient.

We fought for our children in court for over a year, and when we began that process I knew it was going to be difficult, but I never imagined how difficult it would truly become.

I came across an article on a website called *Free From Toxic*. As I was reading it, the things I read were becoming familiar, especially when referring to narcissistic abuse and how they implement a smear campaign. This passage in particular, "…intentional and malicious attacking of the heart, soul, spirit, mind, and often the wallet of another human being cloaked in counterfeit expressions of love and concern."

Sue had ulterior motives from the beginning. To put it in its simplest form she wanted to keep my children and never give them back, all backed by her own selfish agenda. There were no questions as to what was really best for the children. I do not believe she truly cared about them at all.

I want to make this clear: this is my perception. I do not believe this person has empathy, and I believe this person is a wolf in sheep's clothing, masquerading as a loving daughter of Jesus Christ, but in reality lives a life saturated in evil intentions. Again, my opinion. It had come down to a real life *Mommie Dearest*, narcissistic tendencies and all, against Mommy Drunkest, character defects and problems galore. I was told during this time that,

"Nobody believes a drunk." I have found that when someone is telling the truth, and the truth always does come out, that it doesn't matter if they're a drunk or not. The truth is the truth. I have been accused of many things in my life, some I had done and some I had not.

The things these people were accusing me and Jack of were the most awful, disturbing, heinous things, and I could not have imagined even if I tried. This woman knew all about my past, the molestation that happened throughout my childhood. She had the audacity to suggest that I had the potential to treat my own children the same way. Fucking disgusting. She told the prosecuting attorney that Jack had sexually assaulted me in front of the children. That was news to me.

Our past interactions with the prosecuting attorney actually turned out to be a blessing, because he was familiar with us and didn't believe the lies. He didn't press charges. Since that tactic didn't work, Sue then decided she would accuse both Jack and me of sexually abusing our children. I could go off right now and tell you exactly how I feel and what I think about this absolutely disturbing accusation and the accuser. I know better than that, so I've picked out a Bible verse that I had read with regularity during this time and I believe it paints a picture perfect portrait of this woman.

Psalm 5:9
Not a word from their mouth can be trusted;
Their heart is filled with malice.
Their throat is an open grave;
With their tongues they tell lies.

I do not know how I survived this time in my life sober. My only conclusion is that God really did carry me through this. I never could have done it on my own. I finally learned the true meaning of gratitude and I am thankful every day, even when it is difficult. I know there is a never-ending list of people and things for which I am grateful.

I went through my biggest heartbreak, more like a heart loss, all without alcohol, pills, or other substances. The four people I loved the most were gone and my heart went with them. I also came to understand the saying "you don't know what you have until it's gone." I had no idea how truly blessed I had been.

I believe I now have an appreciation for my children that a lot of mothers don't understand. It took complete devastation for me to even attempt to comprehend their absolute preciousness and what a gift they truly are. Even in the tough times, they have always been and will always be my little angels.

To survive I had to detach myself from certain thoughts and memories. I couldn't dwell on the past anymore and I had to set them all free. I had to live in the moment. Moment by moment sometimes. I learned to access the power in the now. I learned a great deal about myself and one of the biggest realizations I had was discovering that I am the problem.

I am my biggest problem. It might sound strange, but that gave me the greatest sense of freedom I have ever felt. Total sobering relief. I learned to trust in God, and that he did in fact, know better than me, what a concept!

I dealt with some heavy stuff during these months away from my children, and so many people carried me. I learned that asking for help is not a weakness. Relying on God takes total strength; it doesn't show weakness as I had previously believed. I knew deep down in my heart that God had not blessed me with four beautiful children only to have them taken away. A lot of people, God, and I believe, my own children, all aided in saving me from myself and in saving my life.

BRITTANY PRIESTLEY

MOMMY DRUNKEST

"There are no beautiful surfaces without a terrible depth."
 -*Friedrich Nietzsche*

CHAPTER NINETEEN

Courtroom Prayer

AFTER SPENDING MONTHS FIGHTING TO have my children returned to me, I knew I had to remain calm and patient. I believed the truth would come out, and the thousands of pages and documents Sue had sent to the Judge and Child Protective Services would not be taken seriously. They were ludicrous. I knew I just had to wait for Sue to hang herself. It was only a matter of time. I knew that God was on my side. I may be just a drunk, but at least I remained honest and open and humble throughout all the proceedings.

I didn't try to mask a malicious heart with words from God and countless attempts at showing what an upstanding citizen I was, like Sue. I knew they would see right through her and know her for what she really was, just as I had realized many years prior. On top of court costs I was paying her child support. I had no problem giving anything for my children, but I always felt like I was paying her to keep my kids from me. All of that money could have gone to something meaningful and good for the children. In my opinion, what was truly best for my children was not important to her agenda. If that had been the case I would've been a part of their lives as well as Jack. Parental alienation was what she wanted. Complete control.

There are so many things that money cannot buy. I lost something irreplaceable, even once I had my children home with me. Time. I can't go back and celebrate any of their birthdays. I can't go back and see Noah on his first day of kindergarten. I can't go back and see them opening up presents on Christmas morning, dressing up for Halloween, learning their ABC's. I can't go back and witness my oldest child, Astrid getting baptized.

These moments in time have come and gone

and will not return. Smiles, laughs, cries, all the memories made that I was not a part of and not allowed to witness. Time lost was one of the hardest things for me to accept. My only solace was knowing we had so many memories ahead of us. We would have many Christmases, Easters, Halloweens, birthdays, laughs, and cries. I will cherish these things, because I have known not having them.

Being away from alcohol and drugs has allowed me to live and enjoy the present moment we are given, that will become tomorrow's memories. Motherhood is not easy, and any mother who is honest will tell you that. Half the time I have no idea what I'm doing, but at least I am trying my best. I am coming from a place of unconditional love. Every decision is made with my children in mind. I am not perfect by any means, but today, I am not Mommy Drunkest. That is enormous progress.

Every time we would have to appear in court I was in a constant state of communication with God. I also brought my amethyst for intuition and to ward off evil spirits. Mainly, I brought it just be able to grip something tightly. It would help as I sat through a lot of unpleasantries and slanderous accusations, but one day, in November of 2018, I sat calmly. We were looking at another few months of complete wastefulness, going back and forth about all the issues we had already gone back and forth with several times.

We hired a different attorney a little over halfway through the proceedings. We weren't getting the results we wanted with the first one. Our new attorney, Charissa Mayes, was and is a complete rock star. I would recommend her to anyone and everyone that needs a driven, compassionate, intelligent attorney. I love her so much and I can never repay her for the work and dedication she put in on behalf of Jack, my children, and myself. I admire her tenacious attitude and she didn't put up with any bullshit. I am privileged to know her on a more personal level, and I trusted in her completely.

In addition to our prior relationships with the prosecuting attorney, Jack and I also had a history with the judge. He had presided over all of my criminal cases, Jack's as well, and he had married us in the very courtroom where we were presently sitting. On this November day, our attorneys, the judge, and the guardian ad litem (who was a court-appointed representative of the children) were sitting in a small room away from us, discussing the fate of my kids' lives as well as my own. What my family would look like in the future. At this point Sue wanted my two older kids to move to the east coast with other family members (on Jack's side of the family) and she wanted to keep the younger two. She wanted to split up my children, which was exactly what I feared would happen if they had gone into foster care. I had no idea what they were discussing. They were in there for at least two hours, and they would come out to speak with us in intervals.

I sat there praying and communicating with God. I asked for His protection and care and that He surround my children, Jack, and myself with love. I asked for Him to show the truth to all parties involved, and I asked Him to please do what was best for my children. I asked Him to forgive me for my past mistakes and my selfishness. I asked for forgiveness for how ungrateful I had always been, not knowing the blessings I had when I had them. I prayed for so much.

I had prayed for these things many times before, but I had to say it again. I asked Him to be there with me, with His Son, and the Holy Ghost. I asked Him to bring all my loved ones that had passed on, my grandmas, my grandpa, my two uncles, Jack's grandparents. I asked Him to bring any guardian angels that would be of help and guidance. Please, if this was to be His will, let my babies come home to me.

As I was praying I got goose bumps that ran all over my body, head to toe. I felt a calmness wash over me. I felt light, that lightness I always searched for by using substances. This lightness came from within and radiated out. I didn't have to turn around. I felt all of those guardian angels sitting behind me. They had always been there to guard and protect me even when I didn't realize it. At this moment I could feel their love radiate in that room. I prayed, "Thank you God. Thank you for so much. I am so grateful for the many blessings I do have, and that I do not deserve. Thank you for this. In the name of Jesus Christ. Amen."

A few minutes later Sue's attorney whispered some things to her that I could not hear and Sue stormed out of the court room. The guardian ad litem, who was a wonderful, fair man with a great love and justice for children, walked over to Jack and me. Both attorneys followed suit. They looked at us and smiled. They told us congratulations. I wasn't able to comprehend why they were saying this.

They told us the children would be ready to meet us at their therapist's office on December 6th. They would be released to us after that session and the guardianship would be terminated. I was in a state of shock. I could not believe what I had just heard. I even asked, "Is this for real?" To which one of them replied, "Yes it is. Don't question it, just enjoy it." I was still flabbergasted. I was not expecting that in any way, shape or form. The power of prayer is strong and true. It took a few days to really sink in. I was infinitely grateful.

I was anxious and excited when Jack and I drove to the therapist's office. The moment I saw them we ran to each other and hugged and kissed. I will remember that feeling forever. My son, Luke whom I had not been able to see for an entire year, was ecstatic. I had so much joy in my heart just seeing all their beautiful smiling faces. When we met with the therapist she commented that it was as if we hadn't spent a day apart from one another. With that comment I knew we would be alright, not perfect, but we had something better then perfection. We had a perfectly imperfect true love. No matter how sick or drunk or high I had been, I had always been loving and affectionate to my children. I was happy to know they remembered that about me. This time my love, a mother's love, had been enough.

# BRITTANY PRIESTLEY

MOMMY DRUNKEST

Growing

All along they had known
The planted seed had time to grow
They dug it deep and buried it low
Due to fear of the unknown
As it was growing it had no light,
Only blurred vision and unclear sight.
To survive the seed had to fight
Even though chances seemed dark as the night.
No matter what obstacles it came across
It never surrendered, and seemed almost lost.
It did anything no matter the cost,
Still it grew up and unknown boundaries were crossed.

BRITTANY PRIESTLEY

But before it's last stretch to reach the top,
It hesitated and suddenly wanted to stop.
The light had been completely switched off
Secretly it still held hope to reach for the top.
It grew to reach the surface
To be with the radiant sun was its true purpose.
It took a long time for the seed to learn this,
Then it peeked through and lost its blindness.
When the time comes, it will understand
Only love and truth lie in these hands.
All its distractions had been its true plan
To show how right this woman is for that man.

MOMMY DRUNKEST

CHAPTER TWENTY

Purpose of God's Impeccable Timing

EVER SINCE I WAS A little girl I had a lot of dreams for myself. Some I kept dreaming about for years and some were short lived. Some I would keep with me always. One of my biggest aspirations and dreams has always been to write a book and become an author.

My youngest and most healthy form of escape was reading and writing. I kept diaries, wrote in journals, and wrote short stories and poems. I read all the time. I loved and still do love authors like

MOMMY DRUNKEST

Ernest Hemingway, Ralph Waldo Emerson, Virginia Woolf, Henry David Thoreau, William Shakespeare, Mark Twain, Harper Lee, Tennessee Williams, J.D. Salinger, Sophocles, Carl Jung, you get the point.

I have always been curious by nature and I wanted to understand how the world worked, what made people act the way they do, different philosophies and beliefs, the meaning of life. So, I read and I learned and I became inspired. I have always had an opened mind and I was on a constant search for answers.

One answer in particular that I found myself searching for most often was: what is my purpose in life? What is my soul's purpose? What has God put me on this earth at this particular time for? I always believed there had to be a reason. I searched and searched exploring many different avenues—psychics, spiritual healers, and the like. I asked God, and I believe he showed me signs, but at those intervals I was in search of other things and too consumed by them to take the time and remember I still had my dreams.

I have had this feeling for a very long time that I was put on earth to heal others and to help in enlightening people, but how, I wasn't too sure. I followed that road and became attuned and certified in Reiki I and Reiki II. I have dealt with energy all my life, always feeling others as my own, the energy of a room, energy of ones that have passed on, dark energies. I thought that would send me in the right direction.

I felt I would stumble upon my purpose at some point along my journey. I believed if I didn't go searching for my purpose, it might find me. I figured the universe or God would show me what I was meant to see.

I'm not sure if I found it, or like I said, it found me. I truly believe that God lead me to a group that I had never heard of called Recovered On Purpose. It was a normal day in December of 2019, and I wasn't doing anything special. I was on my phone scrolling through Facebook.

I follow some recovery humor groups that post inappropriate, truthful, and hilarious things related to recovery. A share or a link popped up in the group. It basically said: if you're in recovery and you want to write a book click here to set up an interview. I am not usually one to click on those types of things, like ever.

For some reason I did. I even answered the

questions on the questionnaire: rate on a scale of 1-10 how important is it for you to write a book? I answered ten; it has always been a dream of mine. There were other questions too, but the other one that got me interested was something along the lines of: how important is it for you to get your message out to help others and to deter future generations from going down the path of addiction? Ten.

At this point I had over 2 ½ years sober. Serving others had become a source of happiness for me. God and I both knew how much I had taken and taken during my addiction. I wanted to give back. I felt that Recovered On Purpose and its message had the possibility of reaching addicts and alcoholics on a much larger scale. I just had a feeling.

I will be honest and open, during this time I was struggling with my own sobriety. I had some things happening in my world that were deterring me from the right path, even though I wanted and needed to go in the right direction. The devil was back, he was tempting, and he was close to home.

I didn't tell anyone about my thoughts of drinking again. I kept it to myself for about three days. If you are in the recovery community, you know that is not a good sign and it is not healthy. I was reverting back to my ideas and beliefs that self-sufficiency was best and that I could handle this predicament on my own. I came close to taking that infamous first drink. I knew that if I did, that would very likely be the end of me. I could not, would not hurt my children by going down that hellish path again.

For some reason, I kept thinking about this interview I had set up with this guy I had no clue about, named Adam Vibe Gunton. I kept thinking if I drink, then I won't be sober. If I'm not sober, I won't be able to talk to this guy I don't even know, about my sobriety.

I almost cancelled my interview a couple of times and I started doubting my decision to even see what this 90 Days From Pain To Purpose thing was all about. Knowing I had set this interview up kept me from making a devastating mistake. That, and prayer, but sometimes I need something more concrete to hold onto, especially when I'm being pulled by darkness and my sight is clouded. That is not something I like to admit, but it's the truth. I did finally tell a few close friends and I told my

Fellowship. I am sincerely grateful to Adam, because he already helped me tremendously before I had even met him. That is a God thing.

We scheduled our interview for the 7th of January. I was skeptical and I am typically not overly trusting of people when I first meet them, but I felt like I could trust him. I liked him, and I told him the reasons behind how I had answered his questions. He said he wanted me to be a part of his program, 90 Days From Pain To Purpose, and that I had filled the tenth and final spot. I gave him my personal information and I remember thinking, "Why in the world am I giving this perfect stranger my information? This could totally be a scam."

It's disturbing how much society intrudes upon our intuition. I thought he was a little intense; I guess passionate is the right word for it. It is usually my instinct to shy away from getting openly excited about things, because I worry that it will turn into embarrassment. I thought Adam might be able to help me to get out of my shell, out of myself where I like to hide, out of my own way.

I already knew he could teach me about writing a book and how to speak in front of people to get my message out. A message that had the possibility to save a life, or deter someone from going down the path I had journeyed down. I could relieve someone of unnecessary pain and heartache.

I had a feeling he could teach me more, and he has taught me a great deal. Being a part of Recovered On Purpose has opened up my eyes and my mind to so many possibilities for my own life, and for the lives of so many others that have suffered from addiction. This movement has allowed me to live up to one of my favorite parts of a prayer, "Relieve me of the bondage of self," that I had tattooed on the back of my neck at eight months sober. I forget about that tattoo all the time, but that verse I always remember. It means so much to me, because I had been so selfish for so long. Serving others is fulfilling and allows me to get out of myself.

I have met some really incredible people, and I have so much admiration and respect for them. I have had a lot of fun and I have laughed a lot, and for that I am grateful. Working on and writing my book, engaging in the Write Your Book In One Month challenge, and learning new things has helped me immensely. Living life on life's terms can be hard, and it has been inspiring to work with people who want to live life full of true purpose. It's been a respite for me and something I can call my own.

I know that God's purpose for me was to be a mother. I knew that from a very young age. I consider motherhood a privilege and my greatest blessing. God has given me a second chance to become the woman and mother I have always wanted to be. I am grateful my children can see for themselves, that any dream they have, can be realized and come true. I am deeply grateful for my purpose of motherhood beyond measure, but I have to stay somewhat sane in order to take care of them to my full potential. I have gained a lot of clarity in my own life.

I now know what I want, and what I don't want. I have discovered what can give me fulfillment, and what cannot. It has been tiring and emotionally draining at times, but I realize that this is what happens as I grow into the best version of myself that I can be. Things worth having and keeping do not always come easily, but when they do, it is truly amazing and wonderful. Today, I am willing to work for that. I have faith that I will for the rest of my life.

I believe Recovered On Purpose has a mission and values that are good and true. It has God written all over it. I am grateful to have found a community that I can relate to on so many different levels. A community of people that makes me know and believe that I am not alone. I pray that someone reads this book and knows they are not alone, that there is someone out there who understands you.

Adam, I appreciate the guidance you have given me on spiritual matters; God, Jesus Christ, and the Holy Spirit. Thank you, Adam, sincerely, for believing in me and dreaming bigger dreams for me than I could ever fathom. Thank you for seeing something in me that I can't quite see myself. You don't know how nice that is.

I hope to be part of your life, your vision, and your mission. I am honored to have you in my life, as my mentor and as my friend. I hope you know how much you and Recovered On Purpose mean to me. How much it will mean for the world and all the people it can touch and save. I am eternally grateful to you and I do love you from the bottom of my ever-healing heart. I know God has blessed you and I pray He continues to always. I am amazed by God for showing me to you, or vice versa, and this movement as part of my purpose in this life. I am grateful for His truly impeccable timing.

MOMMY DRUNKEST

BRITTANY PRIESTLEY

"The world breaks everyone and afterward many are strong at the broken places."
-Ernest Hemingway

About the Author

Brittany Priestley is an author, who has a strong conviction and vision to help those who suffer from addiction, abuse, and trauma. With this book, she hopes to give a voice to anyone who has endured suffering in silence. Brittany believes, whole-heartedly, that when addicts and alcoholics share their stories, it has the power to change, and potentially, save lives. She hopes to end the stigma of addiction in the eyes of the general public.

With a truer understanding of this epidemic, she has faith that more potential sufferers and casualties, both addicts and their loved ones, can and will be avoided.

Brittany is an advocate for recovery and would love nothing more than to aid in healing and serving the masses, through her experience, her strength, and her hope. She wants every single person on this planet, to know and to accept, how worthy they are of a peace that surpasses understanding.

Brittany currently resides in Missouri with her family. Brittany and her four beautiful children are living life and creating memories that they will cherish always. She prays to and plans to live Recovered On Purpose, one day at a time.

To connect with Brittany Priestley, you can message her through her Facebook page or through her Instagram: brittpatkins. If there are any inquiries for speaking engagements in schools, treatment centers, or events, please reach out. Brittany looks forward to serving you.

MommyDrunkestOfficial@gmail.com

Printed in Great Britain
by Amazon